Margaret Macintyre

TEST

TEST THE SPIRITS

An examination of the charismatic movement

C. S. BUTLER

 EVANGELICAL PRESS

EVANGELICAL PRESS
16/18 High Street, Welwyn, Herts, AL6 9EQ, England.

Bible quotations are taken from the New International
Version, Hodder & Stoughton, 1979.

Butler, C. S.
    Test the spirits: an examination of the
    charismatic movement.
    1. Pentecostalism
    I. Title
    270.8'28   BR1644

    ISBN 0–85234–217–9

Typeset by Inset, Chappel, Essex
Printed in Great Britain by Cox & Wyman, Reading

*To Phil — for his friendship
and to Keith — a teacher
under God.*

Acknowledgements

To Walter Chantry, for the help his book
Signs of the Apostles was to me and for
reading the manuscript; to Erroll Hulse
who read the manuscript and passed it to
Evangelical Press; to several friends who
made helpful suggestions, especially Alec
Taylor and Keith Chambers; and to Ann
Jones for typing the manuscript.

Contents

1.
Introduction

The charismatic meeting

The room was full of men in suits, talking in small groups, greeting one another in loud voices. Now and then a 'Praise the Lord!' rang out over the mumble of conversation.

Subtly the atmosphere changed. There was a feeling of expectancy in the air. Suddenly there was a spontaneous burst of applause, which swelled to a crescendo, punctuated with loud cries of 'Hallelujah!' 'Praise the Lord!' and 'Glory!' The applause faded away as quickly as it had begun and one could now hear the undertone of tongues-speaking from many of those present.

The tongues and exclamations of praise died as some-one stood up. Opening his Bible, he shared a brief exhortation on the way the Spirit was moving in our day. As the first man sat down, another stood to his feet and with large gestures shared a story of a brother known to several of those present.

The undertone of tongues swelled up again and here and there someone would rise to his feet and pray. The tongues, as a background accompaniment, bubbled on. The atmosphere of the meeting was becoming more and more electric and exciting and the babble of tongues and prayer was growing louder. Soon some were shouting exuberantly and a forest of arms was raised in praise.

A few of those present had not joined in the noise and enthusiasm, but had sat quietly praying and observing. As the babble died slightly, someone stood up and began to exhort the brethren to 'enter into liberty'. Without actually being named or pointed out, the 'quiet ones' were singled out for criticism. If you did not raise your hands in the air, you were preventing the Spirit from working in you. Raising the arms and 'moving in liberty' were clearly synonymous.

The meeting continued, the atmosphere building steadily to some unknown climax. Many of those present were singing in tongues, perhaps fifty or sixty people, all singing in their own private prayer languages.

Another brother stood and began to speak to the gathering from the Scriptures. This man had been the minister of a denominational church, but had resigned his pastorate and become part of a 'house church'. He and some of the other men were 'apostles' in a growing group of house churches.

One climax followed another during the evening; the atmosphere was hot with excitement. As the excitement grew, men became freer in the way they expressed themselves. Various men testified or exhorted the meeting (mostly the 'apostles'), others 'prophesied' and one shared his experience of smuggling Bibles behind the Iron Curtain. After two hours or so the atmosphere calmed and the meeting drew to a close.

Who were these men, why were they meeting together and what were they doing? They were a group of 'charismatics', that is, Christians who believe that the spiritual gifts mentioned in 1 Corinthians chapters 12 to 14 are still meant to be operating in the church today. Some of these men claimed to be 'apostles' and exerted a powerful influence over their congregations.

They had met together to build one another up in the Spirit, by using the 'gifts of the Spirit'. Most had come from denominational churches (Church of England and Free Churches) and had been influenced in some way to 'seek the baptism in the Holy Spirit'. The evidence that this had happened was 'speaking in tongues', speaking, supposedly, in a language one had never learned. Once a person had received this 'baptism of the Spirit' he (or she) received a 'gift' which was to be used to build up one's fellow Christians. This could be any one of the gifts listed in 1 Corinthians 12, but was likely to be a 'minor' gift — like tongues — to start with. As one grew in experience, maybe other more spectacular gifts, such as healing or casting out of demons, might be manifested.

While not all charismatics would claim that 'apostles' are with us today and not all meetings would be so noisy or 'free', the meeting described above, which I attended in the late 1960s or early 1970s, is fairly typical of what goes on in the movement. (Compare also Arthur Wallis's book, *The Radical Christian*, published by Kingsway Publications Ltd., Eastbourne, in 1981.)

These charismatics are quite sure that God speaks to them directly through the mouth of another brother (or sister) and gives them a sense of personal communication with God which they had previously lacked.

This book will be an examination of some of these claims in the light of the Scriptures by one who spent fourteen years in the charismatic movement.

The 'gifts'

In the New Testament church, according to 1 Corinthians 12, there were a number of 'gifts', or 'manifestations' of the Holy Spirit, in use at that time.

These are listed in verses 8—10 as:

1. the message of wisdom
2. the message of knowledge
3. faith
4. healing
5. miraculous powers
6. prophecy
7. the ability to distinguish between spirits
8. different kinds of tongues (or languages)
9. interpretation of tongues

These are normally recognized by both charismatics and non-charismatics as 'the gifts of the Spirit', although Paul also mentions in verse 28 'those able to help others' and 'gifts of administration'. In the following chapters we shall examine some of these 'gifts' and the claims of the charismatic movement that these gifts are in operation today.

Some charismatics claim that the gifts died out soon after the apostles died and that they have only reappeared in recent days. Others say that the gifts continued to be manifested all through the church age, though the practitioners of these gifts were persecuted. They go on to state that God is now 'pouring out his Spirit on all flesh', that the gifts are now being given their proper place and that by this means the Lord is building up his church, so that when he returns (which will be soon), the church will be that spotless bride of which the Scriptures speak.

We will first of all examine briefly the occurrences of the gifts down the ages, before and after the actual earthly ministry of the Lord Jesus. Later we will go on to discuss the differing views of the gifts current among charismatic and Pentecostal teachers.

Part I   The history

2.
Charismatic phenomena before Christ

In the historical review we will not seek to distinguish between those occurrences which took place in the true church and those which took place within heretical groups.

I realize that these phenomena have been the subject of a number of fine works by evangelical writers, but trust that, as one who spent fourteen years in and around the charismatic movement, my work will contribute something towards the understanding of this so-called 'renewal'.

Evangelicals should no longer be content to sit on the fence over this issue. If the gifts are to be manifested in our day, then we must examine our Bibles and the present phenomena to see if these things are genuine. We must not say, as some do, 'I believe it is all right for those who feel so inclined to follow after the gifts.' Either the gifts are for today and we should *all* seek to manifest our own gift, or the gifts are not for today, in which case the charismatic movement is in error.

The earliest report we seem to have of any extraordinary phenomena is during the captivity of the children of Israel in Egypt related in Exodus chapters 7 and 8. Bible students will be familiar with the contest between Moses and Aaron (representing Jehovah) and the magicians of Egypt (representing probably a whole pantheon of gods). We note that the magicians were able to duplicate the miracles of turning rods into serpents, the changing of water into blood and the bringing up of frogs on the land; but when they attempted to go further they could not, their power being finite, for their 'gods' were finite. They could not compete with the sign-

miracles of the almighty God of Israel and his servant
Moses.

There are other reports in Egyptian writings of 'ecstatic
utterances of a divinely inspired nature'. These were very
likely to have been 'tongues' or 'prophecy'. It seems that
the Egyptians were learned in the magic/occult arts, which
have their 'gifts'. They probably learned these arts from
Babylon.

There is an early account, dated about 1100 B.C., contained in a document called *The Report of Wenamon*, which
tells how a young man, worshipper of the god Amon, 'became
possessed by a god and spoke in an ecstatic language'[1]. It
seems clear from this reference that the young man spoke
in tongues.

The most widely documented accounts of tongues and
heathen prophecy come from the ancient Greeks. Oracles[2]
were common throughout Greece and existed right up until
the early centuries of the Christian era. There were oracles
at Dodonna and Epirus which claimed to prophesy and
communicate with the dead.[3]

The most famous of these oracles was at Delphi and
operated between 550 B.C. and the early years of the
Christian era. Legend has it that the shrine was originally
the house of Python, a male snake. The god Apollo killed
Python and became the possessor of the holy place. The
priestesses retained the name of the original owner of the
shrine and were called Pythia[4]. The oracle, a priestess,
usually sat upon the tripod to prophesy. This reference to
the tripod is a little obscure, but may refer to a rock, which
was referred to as 'Apollo's tripod', or to the tripod held
by an image of the god. 'She will have been brought up in
the atmosphere of the Apolline cult; she certainly would
be a whole-hearted believer in the god's power and in his
willingness to dictate messages to her; the preliminary
ceremonies would have confirmed her belief . . . while in
her abnormal state, the Pythia would speak intelligibly or
otherwise. But her words were not directly recorded by

the inquirer; he was handed a written document supposed to contain what she had said and, in the great days of the oracle, regularly couched in hexameters. Manifestly there was room here for extensive editing or even wholesale forgery . . . [the language was sometimes] so obscure, vague, or ambiguous as to leave room for different interpretations.'[5]

The fourth-century Christian theologian Chrysostom records: '[She] sits upon the tripod of Apollo and thus the evil spirit, ascending from beneath and entering the lower part of her body, fills the woman with madness and she with dishevelled hair begins to play the bacchanal and to foam at the mouth and thus, being in a frenzy, to utter the words of her madness.'[6] Ira J. Martin adds, 'Priests were apparently in attendance to catch her every utterance, and to interpret her cries and babblings whenever they ceased to be coherent.'[7] It is clear that some of these utterances were tongues.

There are numerous stories of the oracles, but one will show the accuracy and the power of this demonic prophet. Croesus, King of Lydia, some five and a half centuries before Christ, had become alarmed at the spreading power of Persia. For advice on how to counteract her rising influence, he turned naturally to the many oracles available. He determined to test a number of the most notable. He sent ambassadors to several oracles and one was dispatched to Delphi. The test was that the messengers were to reckon a hundred days from the date of their departure from the Lydian Court and then to enquire what King Croesus was doing at that moment. When the ambassadors approached the Pythoness, before they could speak she immediately burst into prophecy:

I can count the sands and know the measures of ocean:
I understand the dumb and hear him that speaketh not.
On my sense there stole the savour of a strong-shelled
    tortoise,
Boiling in a cauldron with the flesh of a lamb:
Brass is the couch underneath it and brass the robe laid
    upon it.

The ambassadors hurried home to Croesus, who, upon hearing the message, performed an act of adoration, for on the appointed day, wishing to make the test as difficult as possible, the king had with his own hands cut a tortoise and a lamb to pieces and boiled them together in a brass cauldron covered with a brass lid. Croesus sent gifts to Delphi and came completely under its influence. He consulted the Pythoness about his projected invasion of Persia. She gave the response: 'Croesus, if he crosses the Halys, will destroy a great empire.' He concluded that the oracle had referred to a defeat for Persia. He crossed the stream Halys and suffered a swift defeat at the hands of his Persian enemy. Too late he perceived that the oracle's prophecy was being fulfilled in the destruction of his own empire.[8]

Plato, who lived between 428 and 348 B.C., knew of the gift of tongues. He observed that the speakers had no control over their own minds and did not understand what they were saying. An interpreter was needed. Visions and healings sometimes occurred along with the tongues-speaking. The Greek writers often referred to this phenomenon of speaking in tongues and prophecy as being the result of 'divine possession'.[9] Plato spoke of four kinds of 'irrational experience, the divine madness of love, prophecy, Dionysian ecstasy and poetic intuition'.[10]

Professor S. Angus describes in his book on the mystery religions that 'ecstasy *(ekstasis)* and enthusiasm *(enthusiasmos)*' could be induced by vigil and fasting, tense religious expectancy, whirling dances, physical stimuli, the contemplation of the sacred objects, the effect of stirring music, inhalation of fumes . . . hallucination, suggestion and all other means belonging to the apparatus of the mysteries. These two kindred abnormal states of consciousness . . . are united by Proclus when he speaks of men "going out of themselves to be wholly established in the divine and to be enraptured".'[11]

It should be noted that 'charismatic' phenomena were known in Corinth before the arrival of Paul the apostle. We have seen that the followers of the god Apollo were well acquainted with prophecy and tongues.

The temple of Apollo dominated Corinth, being built, as in many Greek cities, on a hill overlooking the city. It is very likely that the Corinthian converts to Christianity were already familiar with the gifts as practised in the mystery religions. They had been used to the mindless and extravagant behaviour of prophets and tongues-speakers in the religion of Apollo and may have carried on in much the same way when they came into the church. J. N. Darby's note on 1 Corinthians 14:12 is interesting in this respect. His translation of the verse is 'Thus, ye also, since ye are desirous of spirits . . .' The note states: ' "Spiritual gifts", though in sum the sense, deprives the phrase of its force here. As Gentiles, they were in danger of confounding demon's action with the Holy Spirit; and they did not adequately hold the unity of the Spirit but looked for a spirit's power and action to distinguish themselves. The apostle was obliged to point out the difference between demons and the Holy Spirit. But the word further tends to show the reality of a personal spirit acting, though for the Christian there be but one, the Spirit of God.'[12]

It may be that among those Corinthians practising the real gifts some had come in who were mistakenly practising the false gifts which they had exercised while involved with pagan religions. Paul says at the beginning of 1 Corinthians 12, 'You were . . . led astray to dumb idols . . .' (v. 2). 'No one who is speaking by the Spirit of God says, "Jesus be cursed," [had someone blasphemed the name of Jesus, while under the control of one of the false gifts?] and no one can say, "Jesus is Lord," except by the Holy Spirit' (v. 3). Perhaps these misguided people had used these false gifts believing them to be truly spiritual, but had been in a trance-like state similar to what they had experienced when they had been in paganism. The gifts practitioner in paganism and in heretical groups is frequently unable to control the gift; rather, the gift controls the practitioner. In the church 'everything [was] done in a fitting and orderly way' and the believer using the genuine gifts was able to control what he said in a normal manner and even to remain quiet, though he had a message (see 1 Corinthians 14:28–33, 40). This would not invalidate the genuine gifts practised at Corinth, but *would* account for the confusion over the abuse of the gifts which Paul was trying to correct.

3.
The gifts in the New Testament

The list in 1 Corinthians 12:8—10 is taken by the majority of Pentecostal/charismatic teachers to be a comprehensive list of the gifts operating in New Testament times.

These gifts are interpreted by different teachers within the movement in different ways. They are nearly always separated from the fruit of the Spirit (Galatians 5:22—24), although some charismatics do not distinguish between gifts and fruit. It is interesting that two other gifts, those of helping others and of 'administration', are mentioned later in the chapter (v. 28). These two gifts are rarely mentioned by charismatic teachers.

What were all these gifts?

Was the 'message of wisdom' someone simply being given the ability to say something wise at a particular time, or did someone speak with wisdom all the time? What was the difference between the 'message of wisdom' and the 'message of knowledge'? How did the gift of 'faith' operate? It clearly was not ordinary faith; it must have been a special measure of faith given for a particular purpose. Were the gifts only operated in meetings, or could they be performed at all times, even out of the context of a meeting?

It has to be said that, from our considerable distance in time, we just do not know how these gifts operated. In spite of the fact that charismatic teachers claim to know what each gift is, though they do not agree among themselves, there is no clear guidance even in Scripture as to how some of the gifts worked.

It is the gifts of the 'message of knowledge' and 'wisdom', 'faith' and 'miraculous powers' which seem puzzling to us. Were these gifts in any way similar to the present-day phenomena? The charismatic movement would claim that the gifts of the New Testament and the present day variety are the same, though one or two teachers do not agree.

What is clear is that the Lord Jesus performed many signs, miracles and healings during his earthly ministry. The signs and miracles were a sign to the Jews that 'the Prophet' had come to them. Peter said on the Day of Pentecost, 'Jesus of Nazareth was a man accredited by God to you by miracles, wonders and signs, which God did among you through him . . .' (Acts 2:22). The people saw the signs and miracles which Jesus performed and came to the correct conclusion: 'Surely this is the Prophet who is to come into the world' (John 6:14, see also John 7:31).

The apostles also performed signs and wonders, indeed we see that 'God also testified . . . by signs, wonders and various miracles, and gifts of the Holy Spirit . . .' (Hebrews 2:4). These signs, wonders and miracles were the signs of an apostle, for Paul clearly states to the church at Corinth that these gifts were a proof of his apostleship: 'The things that mark an apostle — signs, wonders and miracles — were done among you with great perseverance' (2 Corinthians 12:12).

We shall look at the supposed modern equivalents of some of these gifts in a later chapter.

4.
The phenomena after the New Testament era

The early church

We come now to an examination of gifts and pseudo-gifts after the immediate New Testament period and it will be plain that much of what is written seems to be shrouded in mystery. Even at this early stage of church history the knowledge of the New Testament gifts is not crystal clear.

Justin Martyr (110—165), writing to Trypho, a Jew, says, 'For the prophetical gifts remain with us even to the present time. And hence you ought to understand that [the gifts] formerly among your nation have been transferred to us. Now it is possible to see amongst us women and men who possess gifts of the Spirit of God.' But his definition of these gifts makes it clear that he was not talking about the gifts listed in 1 Corinthians 12. The gifts he referred to were the prophetical gifts to Solomon (spirit of wisdom), to Daniel (spirit of understanding and counsel), to Moses (spirit of might and piety), to Elijah (spirit of fear) and to Isaiah (spirit of knowledge).[1]

Ireneaus (130—202) gives a vivid description of Marcus the magician ministering to a woman for the gift of prophecy: ' "Behold, grace has descended upon thee; open thy mouth and prophesy!" But when the woman would reply, "I have never prophesied and do not know how!" he would begin afresh with his incantations so as to astonish the deluded victim, and command her again, "Open thy mouth, and speak whatever occurs to thee and thou shalt prophesy." She then, vainly puffed up and elated by these words and greatly excited by the expectation of prophesying, her heart beat violently, reaches the requisite pitch of audacity, and idly as well as impudently utters some nonsense as it happens to occur to her, such as might be expected from one heated by an empty spirit. And then she reckons herself a prophetess.'[2]

In the latter part of the second century there arose the movement which became known as Montanism. We might describe this movement as a second-century charismatic movement. Indeed some modern charismatic leaders look upon Montanism as one of the forerunners of the modern movement. (See Michael Harper *As at the Beginning* and Morton T. Kelsey in *Tongue-Speaking: An Experiment in Spiritual Experience.*)

The movement was named after its leader, Montanus (126–180). One tradition says that he was a priest of the Greek goddess Cybele and if this is true, he would almost certainly have been familiar with pagan prophecy and tongues. He added to the teaching of the church and claimed that God's revelation to him was final. He believed in and taught the imminent return of Jesus Christ and the descent of the New Jerusalem onto a plain between the Phrygian villages of Pepuza and Tymion. He taught that the Christian should become passive and allow the Spirit of God to take control of him. Any words spoken in this state were supposed to be the voice of the Spirit. Montanus states, 'Behold man is a lyre and I [he was speaking on behalf of God] hover over him as a plectrum. Man sleeps and I wake; behold it is the Lord who takes away the hearts of men and gives them other hearts.'[3]

'Through his unquenchable desire for leadership [Montanus] gave the adversary opportunity against him. And he became beside himself and, being suddenly in a sort of frenzy and ecstasy, he raved and began to babble and utter strange things, prophesying in a manner contrary to the constant custom of the church handed down by tradition from the beginning.' So states Eusebius of him.[4]

Montanus gave tongues a place of great importance in his churches. He also discouraged marriage. The emphasis on the gifts and the certainty of the imminence of the Second Coming are very similar to the present movement. Tertullian (160–220), the theologian, was a Montanist.

Origen, another early theologian, writing in the middle of the third century, claimed that the charismatic gifts were no longer valid.[5]

Eusebius (264–340), the great historian of the early church, connected prophecy (in the charismatic sense) and tongues, not with the true church, but with heresy and error. 'The false prophet,' he wrote, 'speaks in a trance, which induces irresponsibility and freedom from restraint; he begins by deliberate suppression of conscious thought, and ends in a delirium over which he has no control.'[6]

Chrysostom (345–407), another early theologian and writer, states that the 'gifts of the Spirit' had ceased to function in the church in his time. In his commentary on 1 Corinthians 12 he writes, 'This whole place is very obscure, but the obscurity is produced by our ignorance of the facts referred to and by their cessation, being such as then used to occur but now no longer take place.'[7]

Augustine of Hippo (354–430) is perhaps the best known figure from this early period of the church. He writes, in his comments on the First Epistle of John, 'In the earliest times "the Holy Ghost fell on them that believed and they spake with tongues" . . . these were signs adapted to the times. For there behoved to be that betokening of the Holy Spirit in all tongues, to show that the gospel of God was to run through all tongues over the whole earth. That thing was done for a betokening and it passed away.'[8]

In his *Retractions,* written towards the end of his life he says, 'Those that are baptized do not now receive the Spirit on the imposition of hands, so as to speak in the tongues of all the peoples; neither are the sick healed by the shadow of the preachers of Christ falling on them as they pass; and other such things as were then done are now manifestly ceased.'[9]

John Sherrill, a modern charismatic writer, quotes Augustine as saying, 'We do what the apostles did when they laid hands on the Samaritans and called down the Holy Spirit on them by the laying on of hands. It is expected that converts should speak with new tongues.'[10] However, no source for this quotation is given and it seems unlikely that Augustine would contradict himself so blatantly.

Augustine's views on miracles (particularly healing) seem somewhat puzzling, for while he says that the type of miracles performed in the New Testament had ceased, he quotes in his mammoth volume *The City of God* a number of miracles of healing performed by 'the sacrament', 'by the making of the sign of the cross over the affected part of the body' and miracles performed at the shrines of saints. These miracles cannot be classified as New Testament miracles, to which they bear absolutely no resemblance.[11]

From the writings of this period of the church, that is from Justin Martyr to Augustine, it is very clear that 'the gifts of the Spirit', as recorded in the New Testament, had died out. The only groups practising the 'gifts' were the heretical groups such as the Montanists. There seems little doubt that the church proceeded to go into a state of decline, when those who would today be described as 'evangelicals' became the persecuted minority. However, it is easy to assess from their writings which groups were biblical and which were heretical. It was some of the heretical groups who insisted that the gifts were continuing.

The Middle Ages

During this dark age, we have the high point of those signs and wonders of the Roman church which were looked upon as miracles. These consisted of healings, etc., which took place at the tombs of saints and martyrs, or at those shrines which retained some relic of saint or martyr. These stories continue to the present day — of weeping Madonnas, of vials of the virgin Mary's milk, of vials of the blood of Christ, all of which had miraculous power to heal or to bring some blessing. These superstitious signs and wonders, encouraged by the Roman church, drew her further into that unhealthy and unbiblical position which she attained during the medieval period.

In the eleventh century a German abbess, St Hildegard (1098–1179), reportedly spoke in tongues. These utterances were written down and preserved, but on analysis were found to be a jumble of German, Latin and misunderstood Hebrew. She was, however, called a seeress and prophetess by some of her contemporaries.[12]

Moving into the twelfth century, we meet a character who was to have a profound effect upon a number of 'spiritual' movements in Europe for a number of years. His name was Joachim (often called Joachim of Fioré or Flora). He lived from 1130–1200 and became abbot of a Cistercian monastery in Flora. He displayed great interest in biblical prophecy and was regarded by some, certainly after his death, as a prophet. He claimed that from the ruins of the old, corrupt church would spring a new, spiritual church. Some of his writings were taken up by a Franciscan monk called Gerard. He collected them into one volume called *The Everlasting Gospel*. He declared this work to be the gospel named in Revelation 14:6. The angel in this passage was purported to be Francis of Assisi (1182–1226), the founder of Gerard's order. This 'everlasting gospel' would supersede the New Testament writings in 1260. Joachim propagated the theory of three ages or periods. The first age was the age of the Father, when God revealed himself in fear, power and faith. Then came the age of Christ, the New Testament age, when God revealed himself by the letter of the gospel in humility, truth and wisdom. The last days, the days of the Holy Spirit, would crown everything with perfect love, joy and freedom.[13] This theory has been used since, in varying forms, by many strange groups. Nearly always they date the start of the age of the Spirit from the founding of their own movement.

At about this period we have the appearance of a curious phenomenon — stigmatization. The stigmatic, usually as a result of prolonged prayer and meditation on the sufferings of Christ on the cross, spontaneously produces marks in his or her own body, corresponding to the wounds of the Saviour. These marks, which often bleed profusely, are supposed by devout Roman Catholics to be the fulfilment of Paul's words in Galatians 6:17.

The best known of these stigmatics is undoubtedly Francis of Assisi (1182–1226), but since his time there have been numerous others, up to Padre Pio (a Franciscan monk) in our own day. Since the time of Francis there have been well over 300 cases of stigmata, of which sixty-two resulted in canonization or beatification. The vast majority of these cases seem to have been women. It is taught by the mystics of the Roman church that stigmatics share in the sufferings of Jesus. They '. . . expiate like him the sins of which they are personally innocent . . . (and) redeem sins . . .'[14] These things are clearly signs and wonders, but cannot be said to be biblical. Indeed they are unscriptural and anti-Christian.

Two very well-known Roman Catholic saints, St Dominic (1170–1221) and St Anthony of Padua (1195–1231) are both said to have spoken in tongues.[15] The famous Roman Catholic theologian St Thomas Aquinas (1226–1274), however, believed that tongues had ceased and that anyone who spoke in tongues was demon-possessed.[16]

Around the middle of the thirteenth century (c. 1250), a group called the Begherds came into existence. They looked upon themselves as Franciscans; indeed they are often referred to, along with a number of other groups, as Spiritual Franciscans. As we shall see, they were not particularly spiritual. These people, who were mainly laymen and women, kept a vow of strict poverty. They wandered around Europe begging, sometimes in fairly large groups. At a later stage of their development they formed an alliance with two other similar groups — the Fraticelli and the Brethren of the Free Spirit. Though they were basically Roman Catholic, the

Roman church accused them of licentiousness. Large numbers of women joined the movement. Their headquarters were situated in Cologne and from there they spread along the Rhine into France and the Netherlands. The Roman church issued various decrees and bulls against them and in 1322 the Inquisition was let loose on them.

The movement was Antinomian and attempted to restore the 'divine life of freedom, innocence, and nature. The idea they formed of that state was that man, being in and of himself one with God, requires only to act in the consciousness of that unity, and to follow unrestrained the divinely implanted impulses and inclinations of his nature in order to be good and godly; that prior to the fall he possessed such a consciousness to the full, but that it had been disturbed by that event; that the law had introduced differences among mankind, who originally stood upon a level, but that these ought now to be done away, and the Paradise state of unity and equality restored . . . On such occasions [when they met together] one of their "apostles" came forward and taking off his clothes and exemplifying in his own person the state of innocence, delivered a discourse upon the free intercourse of the sexes, which the law of marriage, contrary to nature, had supplanted. The sequel, if we may credit the reports, was of a kind which forbids description.'[17] The movement was influenced by a number of 'spiritual' writers including Joachim of Flora.

At the beginning of the fourteenth century a group called the White Brethren came into existence. They were named for their white robes, which covered them completely, leaving only eye-holes. Their unknown leader proclaimed that he was the prophet Elias and was come to herald the second coming of Christ. They were eventually dispersed by papal troops after raising an abortive crusade against the Turks. Their leader was burned as a heretic.[18]

St Vincent Ferrier (1357–1419), a Dominican monk who carried out a preaching tour of Western Europe, is credited with performing miracles. Some of his biographers also claim that he spoke in tongues.[19]

The Reformation

It is claimed by Thomas Zimmerman, general superintendent of the Assemblies of God, that Martin Luther (1483–1546) spoke in tongues. He cites this statement from Erich Sauers' *History of the Christian Church*: 'Dr Martin Luther was a prophet, evangelist, speaker in tongues and interpreter, in one person, endowed with all the gifts of the Holy Spirit.' However, no statement from Luther's own writings is cited as proof of this claim. Sauers may have been referring to Luther's ability to speak and read German, Latin, Greek and Hebrew.[20] Luther believed in divine healing and wrote in a letter to a friend in 1545: 'When you depart [from the sick person] lay your hand upon the man again and say, "These signs shall follow them that believe; they shall lay hands on the sick and they shall recover." '[21]

St Francis Xavier (1506–1552), the famous Roman Catholic Jesuit missionary to the Far East, is reported to have spoken in Japanese without previously knowing that language, but other reports stress the difficulty that he had in learning it.[22]

Around the year 1520 a group of German Anabaptists fell into heresy. This group came to be known as the Zwickau prophets or Abecedarians. They claimed that they were directly inspired by God and taught that this inspiration was hindered by any kind of human learning. It was better, they suggested, never to learn the A B C, as all human learning was based upon the alphabet. This kind of knowledge opens the door to that which is an obstacle of the divine illumination. Carlstadt, one of Luther's allies, joined this movement, locked away all his books and even forsook the study of the Bible.[23]

In about the year 1535 a David Joris (or George), who had been a Dutch Anabaptist, started a group with teachings based upon his own visions and revelations. He printed some of these in a *Wonder Book* in 1542. This group became known as the Familists or Family of Love. They maintained that no true knowledge of Christ or the Scriptures could be obtained outside their sect. Moses had taught the law, Christ had taught faith, the Familists taught love. They taught that they had attained to deification by direct communion with God. They spoke of all outside their group as 'ungodded' and 'unilluminated'. They denied the reality of Christ's incarnation and said that they had come to establish the 'Last Days'. They were extreme Antinomians. The sect had two groups, one of which denied that there was any such thing as sin. Not surprisingly, immorality was common among them.[24]

The seventeenth century

In England, during the early days of the Quaker movement in the seventeenth century, a number of instances of charismatic phenomena have been reported. There were certainly prophecies, visions and probably speaking in tongues. Some of the early Quaker prophecies are similar to the present-day phenomenon. The early Quakers, however, seem to have been much more familiar with their Bibles than many charismatics. The Quaker attitude to Scripture was not evangelical; they maintained, for example, that several books were missing from our Bibles, including the Book of Enoch and the Third Epistle to the Corinthians. They believed that the Bible 'was only a secondary rule, subordinate to the Holy Spirit. Experience therefore sat in judgement upon the Bible.'[25] This latter error we shall come across again in our examination of the modern movement.

A Roman Catholic group called the Jansenists appeared in France in the seventeenth century. This group claimed that 'experience, not reason, was their guide'. They did not believe in justification by faith. Tongues-speaking took place in this group which was later condemned by Rome.[26]

Their successors, who became known as the Convulsionnaires, spoke in tongues while in an unconscious state and remembered nothing when they returned to a normal state.[27]

This movement sprang from the Jansenist sect. At the grave of a Jansenist priest named Paris, a cripple was reported to have been healed. Epileptics and sick people crowded the cemetery seeking a miracle. Sympathizers were seized with convulsions. The local Roman Catholic dignitary Cardinal Noailles insisted that all cures should be registered and this seemed to increase the fame of the shrine. Prophecy began to be manifested as well as healings. Many of the Convulsion-naires were women and some were only children. As the sect grew more and more fanatical, the Convulsionnaires began to indulge in self-torture (a phenomenon that has appeared from time to time in the Roman church), consisting of scorching, scourging and the dropping of boulders upon one another. The movement was eventually stamped out by the authorities.[28]

Another group which started in France during the same period were the Camisards of the Cevenne region. These Huguenots (French Calvinists) rose in rebellion to resist the tyrant Louis XIV. They were subjected to great persecution and a prophetic movement seems to have sprung up as a result of their hardships. Their leaders were chosen for their spiritual gifts. 'They had a complete system of spiritual gifts and grades; innumerable prophets arose among them; ecstasies and trances were frequent, and the wildest utterances that could be prompted by misery, distress, and privation were regarded as the teachings of the Spirit.'[29] Their gift of tongues took place while the speaker was in a trance, the person often swooning and gasping for breath. The predictions that came through the gift of prophecy were not fulfilled. Due to the extreme persecution in France many fled to England and sought to join the Moravians and Methodists. In England they became known as the French Prophets. John Wesley rejected them as 'a set of enthusiasts', whose 'imaginary inspirations contradicted the law and the testimony'.[30]

Early Methodism and the Great Awakening

John Wesley (1703–1791), one of the founders of Method-
ism, acknowledged that spiritual gifts were not in evidence
in his day. He said, 'The cause of their decline was not, as
has been vulgarly supposed, because there is no more need
of them, because all the world were become Christians . . .
the real cause was: the love of many, almost all Christians
so called, was waxed cold . . . this was the real cause why
the extraordinary gifts of the Holy Ghost were no longer
to be found in the Christian Church: because the Christians
were turned heathen again and had only a dead form left.'[31]
Wesley had to contend in his societies with 'enthusiasm',
which had features in common with the charismatic movement. Of these 'enthusiasts' John Wesley wrote that they
took 'their own imaginations for impressions from God . . .
fancying . . . that they had the gift of prophecy, and of discerning of spirits'.[32] John Wesley is often quoted as an ally
by present-day charismatics, because of his remarks already
quoted on the gifts. Therefore it is interesting to note that
when he did come across a group which claimed the gifts
of the Spirit, he dismissed them as 'enthusiasts'. Wesley can
be regarded as a forerunner of the modern Pentecostal and
charismatic movements. He taught a second blessing, which
in Pentecostalism developed into 'the baptism of the Holy
Spirit'. We shall come across his influence again later on.

Roughly contemporary to Wesley, a completely unrelated
group came into existence among the Jews of Eastern Europe.
Israel Ben Eliezar (1699–1761) had various religious
experiences and in 1735, because of his miraculous cures,
became known as Baal Shem Tov. This title means 'Master
of the Divine Name' and was conferred on those who had
proved that they could perform miracles in the name of
God. The movement, known as Hassidism, spread throughout
Eastern Europe among pious Jews. The religion that Baal
Shem Tov taught was a Jewish mysticism. Purity of heart
was superior to study, and prayer and the keeping of the

commandments were encouraged. The worship was accompanied by spontaneous dancing and singing. There are many tales of signs, miracles, healings and visions and of extraordinary prophetic insight. The leadership was conferred on pious leaders and sometimes passes through particular families.[33] The migration of Jews to the West brought Hassidism with it and it has a large number of adherents in New York. The leading figure in Western Hassidism, though he was by no means an orthodox Hassid, was the late Martin Buber (1878–1965). He was born in Vienna and came under the influence of Hassidism early in his life. He interpreted this form of Judaism for the West, his most famous book being *I and Thou*. Buber saw religious faith as a dialogue between man and God and the Bible as a record of that experience. Israel knows herself to be addressed by God and tries to respond, that is, to listen and to obey.

In America, during the Methodist period in the United Kingdom, there was revival under the ministry of Jonathan Edwards (1703–1758). Edwards and other pastors who watched over the converts constantly warned them against 'fanaticism'. The 'fanatics' looked to impressions, trances, visions and revelations, but where these occurred they were crushed by responsible leaders. The main error was the conclusion that outward appearances (visions, revelations, etc.) were an indicator of the depth of inward spiritual experience.[34] Edwards says that when the Spirit of God moved upon people he affected them in two ways: 'One was, that they have . . . immediately . . . quit their sinful practices; and the looser sort have been brought to forsake and dread their former vices and extravagancies . . . The other effect was that it put them on earnest application to the means of salvation, reading, prayer, meditation, the ordinances of God's House, and private conference.'[35]

One fanatic who caused great problems for Edwards and other pastors was James Davenport. When he had been delivered from following a subjective guidance, he wrote a moving confession which contains the following paragraph:

'I confess I have been much led astray by following impulses or impressions as a rule of conduct, whether they came with or without a verse of Scripture; and my neglecting also duly to observe the analogy of Scripture. I am persuaded this was a great means of corrupting my experiences and carrying me off from the Word of God, and a great handle, which the false spirit has made use of with respect to a number, and me especially.'[36]

Shortly after the revival under Edwards and Whitefield a movement sprang up which became known as the Shakers. This sect originally began in Britain among a group of Quakers who had been influenced by the Camisards. The movement started in about 1747 and its first leader was a woman called Jane Wardley. In 1770, Ann Lee (1736–1783), daughter of a Manchester blacksmith, was made leader. Her title was 'Spiritual Mother in Christ' and she was known thereafter as Mother Lee. She professed to work miracles and speak in tongues. In 1776 she and a group of followers emigrated to America and formed a settlement near Albany. The number of followers increased rapidly. Ann Lee died in 1783 and, though the sect continued, it is now a small band of eccentrics with no power or influence. An eyewitness account by a Dr Dwight describes them as singing in an unknown tongue. The doctor describes it as 'a succession of unmeaning sounds frequently repeated, half articulated, and plainly gotten by heart, for all uttered the same sounds in succession . . . They practised many contortions of the body and distortions of the countenance.'[37] Ann Lee taught that Jesus was not the incarnate God-man and that she herself was the fulfilment of Christ's second coming. She also described herself as 'Ann the Word'.[38] There were also manifestations of clairvoyance, telepathy, prophecy, singing, dancing and possession by departed spirits.[39]

Another group claiming special revelations and gifts of prophecy were the followers of Joanna Southcott (1750–1814). She was born in Devon, a farmer's daughter, and

was naturally religious. She was brought up as an Anglican but
became a Methodist in 1791. In 1792 she began to write a
book of prophecies which was described as 'incoherent in
thought and grammar'. In 1813 she claimed that she was
pregnant by the Holy Ghost with a child which would be
called Shiloh. She died of unknown causes the following
year and when examined after death was found not to be
pregnant. She left a box in which, it was claimed, would
be the answer to the the country's problems. It was to be
opened by twenty-four bishops of the Church of England.
A box was opened in 1927, but it was found to contain only
trivia. However, the present-day followers of this strange
sect claim that there is another, true box which has not
been opened. They advertise in the national press from time
to time under the name of the Panacea Society.

Edward Irving and his followers

We come now to a sect which came from the surprising background of Scottish Presbyterianism. This movement has had
some influence on the present-day movement. Edward Irving
(1792—1834) was a minister of the Presbyterian Church in
London. He seems to have been influenced by two men:
firstly, J. S. Stewart, who desired to see an outpouring of
the Holy Spirit upon Scotland, and, secondly, Henry
Drummond, who had organized a number of meetings for the
study of prophecy. Irving came to believe that the charismata
(as recorded in 1 Corinthians 12—14) belonged to all ages
of the church and were only absent due to the want of
sufficient faith.

In Scotland Mary Campbell and a number of others had
been influenced by the sermon of a Mr A. J. Scott on the
charismatic gifts. This inspired them to pray for the restoration of the gifts.[40] At a meeting held around the bed of a
sick girl, a prophecy was uttered that there would be a mighty
outpouring of the Spirit. When this young lady's twin

brothers, James and George McDonald, came home from work, she told them of her feeling about the coming of the Spirit and prayed that James would be endued with the power of the Holy Ghost. Almost immediately, James said calmly, 'I have got it!' He went to his sister's bedside and said to her, 'Arise and stand upright.' Repeating the words he took her by the hand and she arose. James then wrote to Miss Mary Campbell, who was also sick, commanding her in the name of the Lord to arise. Mary wrote later, 'I was made verily in a moment to stand upon my feet, leap and walk, sing and rejoice.' Later, on a March Sunday morning, Mary, in the presence of some friends, started to make incomprehensible sounds. She believed this to be the gift of tongues. She endeavoured to find out what this tongue was, so that she might become a missionary, if the Lord strengthened her. She eventually announced that it was the language of a group of islands in the South Pacific. It is not revealed how she reached this conclusion and she never became a missionary.

Edward Irving recorded some of the tongues spoken at this time and a deputation from his London congregation travelled to Scotland to experience the gifts at first hand. When they returned to London, prayer meetings were organized by Irving and several evangelical ministers 'to seek of God the revival of the gifts of the Holy Ghost in the church'. The meetings started towards the end of the year 1830 and by 30 April 1831 one of the wives of the men who had been to Scotland had spoken in tongues. This outburst of tongues-speaking was reported publicly in October 1831. There was even a report about it in *The Times*. At the public meeting on the evening of 16 October 1831 a Mr Taplin delivered a tongues message, ending in English with: 'Oh, Britain, thou anointed of the Lord! Thy destruction is at hand! Fear not, ye people of God.' Irving wrote to his father-in-law that God '. . . has raised up the order of prophets amongst us, who, being filled with the Holy Ghost, do speak with tongues and prophesy'.

Irving was eventually expelled from the Scottish Kirk for two reasons: firstly, that he held that the human nature of Christ was capable of sin, and, secondly, an account of the 'manifestations' taking place in his church. He and his congregation moved to a church in Newman Street and resumed their meetings.

After having been away on one occasion, he was informed on his return by one of his 'apostles' that he was to suspend his preaching and the administration of the sacrament until he received a new ordination. He was soon reinstated as 'angel' over the Newman Street congregation. However, his ministry faded and he took less and less part in the meetings. He died in 1834 at the age of forty-two. He had never experienced the satisfaction of speaking in tongues himself and the movement which his preaching had helped to start overtook him.[41]

The Irvingites gradually developed into the Catholic Apostolic Church. They restored the position of twelve 'apostles' and developed into a sort of popeless Romanism, embracing such things as transubstantiation, extreme unction, candles, incense, holy water, choral services, capes and vestments, decorated altars and so on. The sect, like many other charismatic groups, has now almost ceased to exist.

It is interesting to note that the Irvingites taught that there were two kinds of tongues — 'Pentecostal tongues', which were foreign languages, and 'Corinthian tongues', which were ecstatic, unknown languages. Only the Corinthian variety were practised among them. Irving made the following comment on tongues: 'When the speech utters itself in the way of a spiritual song, it is the likest to some of the most simple and ancient chants in the cathedral services, insomuch that I have often been led to think that those chants, of which some can be traced as high as the days of Ambrose, are recollections and translations of the inspired utterances in the primitive church.'[42]

A premillennial writer has gone so far as to suggest that the origin of the pre-tribulation rapture view was given in a tongues message through a woman in an Irvingite meeting.[43]

Irvingite prophecy was frequently recorded and, in the few examples I have seen, we see the shallowness, the misunderstanding of Scriptures and the plain silliness of the movement. What are we to make, for example, of the prophecy already quoted, which speaks of Britain as the anointed of the Lord? It is a blasphemous nonsense.

Here are some other examples:

'Oh! you do grieve the Spirit — you do grieve the Spirit! Oh! the Body of Jesus is to be sorrowful in Spirit! You are to cry to your Father — to cry, to cry, in the bitterness of your souls! Oh! it is a mourning before the Lord, — a sighing and crying unto God because of the desolations of Zion — because of the desolations of Zion — because of the desolations of Zion!'

'Oh! Grieve Him not! Oh! Grieve not your Father! Rest in His love! Oh! Rejoice in your Father's love! Oh! Rejoice in the love of Jesus! In the love of Jesus! Oh! For it passeth knowledge! Oh! the length! Oh! the breadth! Oh! the height! Oh! the depths of the love of Jesus! Oh! It passeth knowledge! Oh! rejoice in the love of Jesus! Oh! sinner! for what, for what, what, oh! sinner can separate, separate, separate from the love of Jesus! Oh! nothing, nothing, nothing! Oh! none shall be able to pluck you out of your Father's hands.'

'Ah! be ye warned! be ye warned! ye have been warned! The Lord hath prepared you a table, but it is a table in the presence of your enemies. Ah! look you well to it! the city shall be building — ah! every jot, every piece of the edifice. Be faithful each under his load; but see that ye build with one hand, and with a weapon in the other. Look to it! Ye have been warned. Ah! Sanballat! Sanballat! Sanballat! The Horonite! The Moabite! The Ammonite! Ah! confederate! confederate! confederate! with the Horonite! Ah! look ye to it! look ye to it!'[44]

The Mormons

Meanwhile, in America, Joseph Smith (1805–1844) was busy founding his own Mormon Church, more correctly called the Church of Jesus Christ of Latter Day Saints. Joseph Smith himself is reputed to have spoken in tongues. Certainly Article 7 of his summary of doctrine states, 'We believe in the gift of tongues . . . and . . . the interpretation of tongues.'[45] Tongues among the early Mormons were organized, someone being detailed to bring a tongues message: 'Father so-and-so, rise in the name of Jesus Christ. Make some sound without thought, continue to make sounds and the Lord will make a language from them.'[46]

In the *Book of Mormon* (Moroni 10:9–20) there is a list of spiritual gifts, which includes tongues and interpretation of tongues, very similar to the list found in 1 Corinthians 12. However, there are some rather strange additional gifts; for example, the gift of beholding angels and ministering spirits (v. 14). The section concludes, 'I would exhort you . . . that you remember that he is the same yesterday, today, and for ever, and that all these gifts of which I have spoken, which are spiritual never will be done away, even as the world shall stand, only according to the unbelief of the children of men.' These words have a strangely familiar ring to them.

Other nineteenth-century movements

In America, at the same period as the beginning of the Mormon movement, there were reports of outbreaks of tongues following a 'Revivalist' campaign between 1841 and 1843. People had seizures and swore horribly. When the tongues ended, the speaker had little or no memory of what had occurred.[47]

A number of outbreaks of tongues were reported in various places during this period – in Sweden among the Readers

(1841–1843), during the Irish revival (1859), in England after a D. L. Moody campaign (1873), in Switzerland, Estonia and Germany (1885), and among Seventh Day Adventists (1875).

The second-blessing movement

At the end of the nineteenth century there was an increase in the preaching of a second blessing for Christians after conversion. Books were also widely used in the promotion of this teaching. One of the exponents of this doctrine, which was a continuation of the doctrine of 'entire sanctification' taught by the Wesleys, was a South African Dutch Reformed minister, Andrew Murray (1828–1917). Murray writes in *The Master's Indwelling*, 'A man may be an earnest Christian; a man may be a successful worker; a man may be a Christian who has had a measure of growth and advance; but if he has not entered this fulness of blessing, then he needs to come to a second and deeper experience of God's saving power ...'[48] Murray called this experience 'the baptism or fulness of the Spirit'.[49] Many of Andrew Murray's students became Pentecostals. Knowledgeable Pentecostals and charismatics pay tribute to Murray as a forerunner of the modern gifts movement.

In England as a result of a personal crisis Canon Harford-Battersby, an Anglican clergyman, called a convention in his parish of Keswick in 1875. The canon claimed that he had attained a rest and victory over sin as a result of a second blessing. Thus the Keswick or Higher Life Movement was born and in many respects prepared the way for later Pentecostalism.

Some well-known evangelicals were not swayed by the growing emphasis on second blessings and modern-day miracles. The great and mighty preacher C. H. Spurgeon (1834–1892) said, '[Jesus] sent [the disciples] forth to work miracles as well as to preach. Now, he hath not given us this power, neither do we desire it: it is more to God's glory that

the world should be conquered by the force of truth than by
the blaze of miracles.[50]

The Armenian persecution

In Kara Kala, Armenia, a district of Turkey, an event took
place in the mid-nineteenth century which was to have reper-
cussions later in our story and which was to link the Old
World (Europe) with the New World (the United States) and
Pentecostalism with the charismatic movement. Around the
year 1855 (no one seems sure of the exact date), an illiterate
eleven-year-old boy, Efim Gerasemovitch Klubniken, felt
called by God to a week of prayer and fasting. During this
time he saw a number of visions which he wrote down,
copying the form and shape of the letters, pictures and
diagrams he saw. This manuscript was later taken to people
who could read. It turned out to be detailed prophecy. The
Turks, who were Muslims, would turn against the Christian
Armenians and murder them. The Christians were told to go
to the U.S.A. and settle there to escape the massacre.[51]
A second prophecy was given later, which has been kept in
a sealed envelope by the prophet's family. Anyone who
opens this envelope, who is not the one anointed by God to
do so, will die.[52]

Efim announced in 1900 that the first prophecy was
about to be fulfilled and between 1900 and 1912 many
Armenian families emigrated to the U.S.A. and settled on
the west coast. In 1914, at the commencement of the First
World War, the Turks began the systematic liquidation of the
Armenian population. Over a million were driven into the
Mesopotamian desert, another million were massacred in
their villages, including the remaining inhabitants of Kara
Kala.[53] A total of three million were killed.[54] One of the
families which left Kara Kala in the early part of this century was the Shakarians, Pentecostal Presbyterians who
came into contact with the Azuza Street Mission in Los

Angeles, which we will come across in the chapter on the Pentecostal movement.

During the year 1896, a Baptist pastor, Richard Spurling, led a 'revival' campaign in North Carolina. This campaign was marked by an extensive outburst of speaking in tongues.[55]

5.
Pseudo-gifts in modern non-Christian religions

It is perhaps not common knowledge that gifts are in operation in many religious groups throughout the world. These groups may have slight knowledge of Christianity; some do not.

Among primitive, animistic tribes in the more remote regions of the world, these phenomena occur quite frequently. Most of us are aware, from books, television, and so on, that the witch-doctor, shaman, or medicine man still holds a place of power in primitive cultures, sometimes in spite of contact with and supposed adherence to Christianity. We are aware that witch-doctors are able to 'cure' disease and, although this may be in the realm of primitive psychology, it does, to patient and spectator, appear to work. It is also known that the peculiarly Pentecostal gift of tongues is extremely common, a fact not known to many charismatics.

Witnesses reveal that tongues have been known among the Indians of North America, Eskimos,[1] Lapps, Yakuts, Tungus and Samayeds (three of the ancient tribes of Siberia), North Borneo, Micronesia and the Solomon Islands (in the Pacific), Ghana, China, among the Zulus of South Africa, the Segeju of Tanzania, the Luganda in Uganda, the Bantu of Kenya and in Malaya. This list is not exhaustive, but gives some idea of the widespread non-Christian use of this 'gift'. Tongues-speaking also occurs in the Islamic mystical sect of the Sufis and among the Muslims of India.[2]

Perhaps the most astonishing testimony of this phenomenon is from a graduate of Wheaton College in the

U.S.A. This man had been brought up on the Tibetan border, the son of missionary parents. He 'tells of hearing Tibetan monks in their ritual dances speak in English with quotations from Shakespeare, and in German and French'.[3]

Modern spiritualism also displays charismatic phenomena. The modern outburst of spiritualism started in America in 1848. Two sisters, Margaret and Kate Fox (twelve and nine years old respectively), disturbed by tappings and noises in their bedroom, had devised a means of communication with the author of the noises. Upon investigation by a group of adults, these communications developed into a comprehensive system which included messages given with an alphabet. This movement grew so rapidly that by 1871 there were reported to be between eight and eleven million supporters of spiritualism in the U.S.A. alone.[4] Spiritualism has grown apace since then in most parts of the world. There are even some groups who call themselves 'Christian Spiritualists'. Healings, prophecies, visions and manifestations of many kinds take place in spiritualism, including speaking in tongues. The languages of most of the ancient and modern societies are spoken and also Martian and Saturnian![5]

6.
The rise of modern Pentecostalism

Though there are some who would trace the rise of modern Pentecostalism to Edward Irving in the 1830s, most scholars of the movement would date it somewhat later.

In 1900, in the U.S.A., a Methodist evangelist, Charles Parham (1873–1929), founded a Bible school in Topeka, Kansas. The only book allowed in this school was the Bible and corporate prayer was also emphasized. Students took three-hour watches in a 'prayer tower' and there were sometimes whole nights of prayer. Parham opened the school and immediately set his students 'the task of discovering what was the biblical evidence for the baptism in the Holy Spirit'. He had to leave to take meetings in Kansas City, but when he returned he found the students greatly excited. They had examined the New Testament and had come to the firm conviction that the evidence of the baptism in the Spirit was speaking in tongues. They started to pray that they would be baptized in the Spirit as on the Day of Pentecost. One of the students, a girl called Agnes Ozman, asked Parham to lay hands on her, as she recalled three occasions on which this had been done in the New Testament. Parham did as he was requested and as he laid hands on her head, 'A glory fell upon her, a halo seemed to surround her head and face.' She began to 'speak in tongues'. A number of others, including Parham, had similar experiences. They were, however, not accepted by their friends and neighbours; indeed they were often treated as fanatics. Parham is often referred to as 'the father of modern Pentecostalism'.[1]

In 1904 a revival broke out in Wales. Evan Roberts, a coal miner, was prominent among the preachers of this revival. He would get the people in the meetings to pray for the out-pouring of the Holy Spirit, repeating a prayer after him. Roberts corresponded with a number of different people throughout the world who would later become prominent in the soon-to-be-formed Pentecostal churches. One of Roberts' correspondents was a Frank Bartleman of Los Angeles. Bartleman was to become the historian of the early days of the Pentecostal movement in the U.S.A.

Bartleman met W. J. Seymour, an ordained holiness' preacher, a Negro who had been to a college opened by Charles Parham in Houston, Texas. Seymour offered himself for meetings in a Negro church in Los Angeles but was barred and began meetings in North Bonnie Brae Street, where some experienced the 'baptism in the Spirit'. When the neighbours complained about the noise, the meetings moved to Azuza Street to an old livery stable, used at one time as a Methodist church. So started the famous Azuza Street Mission. It is said that meetings lasted here for three years, running day and night non-stop, people coming and going as they were able. It is from this inauspicious location that the teaching spread which became known to the world as Pentecostalism. The meetings were led by men and women preachers. Though Seymour was the mission's chief figure, he preferred to leave the running of the meetings 'to the Holy Spirit'. He often used to sit with his head hidden inside an empty crate.

The Spirit of God was 'seen' falling upon people. Arno Gaebelain, writing in 1907, quoted an extract that he copied from the Azuza Street magazine: 'The power of God fell and everyone was caught up in the Spirit and saw visions of God. Several had a vision of the Saviour. He held a book in His hand. They saw the nail-prints and the blood trickling down while He wrote their names in the book with His fingers with the blood that ran from His pierced hand.'[2] Some who came to preach ended up flat on the floor on their faces, unable to say anything — as Frank Bartleman put it, they were 'dying out'.

In 1905, T. B. Barrett (born 1862), an English Methodist
whose parents had moved to Norway, went to New York
to seek funds for the Oslo City Mission, for whom he worked.
He seems to have been a deeply emotional man and had for
some time prior to his American trip been seeking a 'baptism
of fire'. He had corresponded with Evan Roberts, the Welsh
revivalist. Barrett stayed with Dr A. E. Simpson and while
there read the life of Charles Finney, the American revivalist.
In the meantime his fund-raising was going badly; as he wrote
later, 'All the trials I had passed through during the last
year . . . brought me down, deeper down before the Lord,
seeking, praying, weeping . . .' He was in correspondence
with people at Azuza Street and on Saturday, 7 October
1906 he locked himself in his room for a day of fasting and
prayer. At 5 p.m. he writes, 'I was seized by the Holy Power
of God throughout my whole being and it swept through
my whole body as well . . .' However, he did not speak in
tongues and his friends at Azuza Street, to whom he wrote
describing his experience, told him that he should seek until
he could speak in tongues. On 16 November, Barratt received
the gift of tongues for which he had longed. Someone saw a
crown of fire over his head and a cloven tongue of fire in
front of it. In December he sailed back to Oslo and a stormy
reception from his mission. He eventually founded the Pentecostal Church in Oslo in 1916.[3] Later in his life, because of
some of the experiences that he had had, Barratt came to
believe that 'Other spirits could speak in tongues, by the
power of suggestion.'[4]

In 1907 there was a Pentecostal outbreak in Sunderland,
England, in the Church of England parish of Rev. A. A.
Boddy. Boddy became vicar in 1886 and remained there until
1922. He was an enthusiastic supporter of the Keswick Convention and when the Welsh revival broke out in 1904—5 he
visited Evan Roberts. He was also familiar with T. B. Barratt
and had visited him in Oslo. Boddy persuaded Barratt to
visit Sunderland and during this visit three members of
Boddy's church spoke in tongues. Meetings ran from August

1907 until the middle of October. People came from all over Britain to experience revival and speaking in tongues. Boddy remained in the Church of England until his death, but, partly due to the First World War, Pentecostal groups began to form, separate from the established church. Boddy took no further part in the movement and the leadership of the Pentecostal churches passed to men like Smith Wigglesworth, who had been led into 'a pentecostal experience' at Sunderland.[5]

Smith Wigglesworth (1869–1947) had been a plumber in Bradford, Yorkshire. He was brought up, as so many people are, in the Church of England. As a boy of thirteen he joined the Methodists and, because they seemed to lack the 'fire' that he desired, he went to the Salvation Army. After experiencing healing from peritonitis he embarked upon a healing ministry and eventually went to Sunderland, where he had 'a pentecostal experience and spoke in tongues'.[6] He went on to become a leading figure (if somewhat controversial) in the Pentecostal movement and influenced other leading figures in the movement.

In Maesteg, Wales, Stephen (a miner) and George Jeffreys (who worked in the Co-op) had a Pentecostal experience and later founded the Elim Foursquare Pentecostal Church.[7] Between the two World Wars Stephen Jeffreys held huge evangelistic and healing meetings in the Albert Hall in London. It was said that, as he walked down the aisle, people would be healed quite spontaneously without any physical contact or individual prayer. This is a claim made for a number of Pentecostal healers and there have been odd reports of this phenomenon down the ages. What puzzles me is that these things only seem to occur in special 'healing' meetings. The Lord Jesus and the apostles very often performed their miraculous healings out in the street.

In 1921, in Los Angeles, California, Aimée Semple McPherson founded the International Church of the Foursquare Gospel. This had no connection with the Jeffreys brothers' organization mentioned above. David Christie-

Murray writes that the 'English variety of Pentecostalism . . . was bred out of puritanism by ecstasy' and the methods of Sister Aimée were bred out of 'Hollywood publicity methods'.[8] While the latter would seem fair comment, many followers of the Puritans would disagree with the former sentiment. Aimée Semple McPherson was a controversial figure who made her 'church' into a big business enterprise. She was one of the first 'evangelists' to use the radio to influence the masses. By 1955 the Foursquare Gospel Church had grown to a membership of 63,000 in 604 churches.[9]

During the 1920s and 1930s an American-based Pentecostal mission carried out an effective mission in Eastern Europe and by 1930 there were 350 Assemblies of God churches with a membership of 80,000. In Poland there were 500 Assemblies of God by 1939.[10]

In 1939 a conference took place in England to try to formulate a scheme for unity among the different Pentecostal churches. This conference (followed by another in 1940 and a European gathering in 1939) failed to agree on a common doctrine of the baptism in the Spirit.

The four differing views were:

1.   The seeker should pray for the baptism in the Holy Spirit with signs following. *One* of the signs may be tongues.

2.   The seeker's baptism in the Holy Spirit is *proved* by the sign of tongues. The one baptized *may* never speak in tongues again.

3.   The *sign* of tongues is different from the *gift* of tongues. The *gift* enables the speaker to talk in tongues whenever the Spirit leads him to do so.

4.   Tongues are not a proof of the Spirit baptism. A Christian may produce tongues without the baptism.[11]

In 1939 there were two dozen Pentecostal groups in the U.S.A., with a membership of about 250,000. By 1955 there were thirty-five denominations with nearly 1,500,000 members.[12] By 1962 the Assemblies of God were represented in some seventy-six countries. In Brazil alone there are some 2,000,000 Pentecostals and in Sao Paulo they boast a church which will hold 25,000 people.[13] This used to be proclaimed as the largest church in the world, but is now probably surpassed by the church of Dr Cho in Seoul, Korea. He has 150,000 members in his church.[14]

Pentecostalism has risen from humble beginnings to a place of considerable power in the world.

7.
The rise of the charismatic movement

We come now to Pentecostalism in its more modern form —
variously referred to as 'the charismatic movement', 'the
charismatic renewal' or 'neo-pentecostalism'.

It would appear that the charismatic movement has taken
over the role of the ecumenical movement. A leading charismatic, Harold Bredesen, has written, 'During the first half
of the twentieth century we saw the Holy Spirit breaking
down the walls between the churches, and called it the
"ecumenical movement". We saw him at work alongside the
historic churches and called it "the third force". Now in the
second half of the century, we are seeing him more within
the churches. We call it the "charismatic movement".'[1]

A man called Demos Shakarian seems to have been one
of the first to take 'historic' Pentecostalism into a wider
sphere. Demos Shakarian is the grandson of an American
Presbyterian Pentecostal family who left Turkey as the result
of a 'prophecy' given within the American community (see
chapter 4). The Shakarian family had established themselves
in California, set up a dairy business and through hard work
had become very wealthy. During the late 1940s or early
1950s Dr Charles Price (a well-known Pentecostal minister
with a healing ministry) prophesied to Mr Shakarian: 'You
will witness one of the major events foretold in the Bible.
Just before Jesus returns to earth, God's Spirit is going to
descend on all flesh.' Dr Price had insisted that what God
was going to do would involve laymen rather than ministers.
The emphasis would not be on theologians or clergy or 'great

gifted preachers, but men and women with ordinary jobs in the ordinary world'.[2]

Mr Shakarian believed that God was leading him to start some sort of outreach where people would simply be able to testify to one another to what God had done for them. Doctrine was not to have any place in these meetings. In 1951, with the well-known Pentecostal evangelist and T.V. personality Oral Roberts, Demos Shakarian founded the Full Gospel Businessmen's Fellowship International, to put this idea into action.[3] The FGBMFI technique is to organize a luncheon or dinner and invite along local businessmen. Various speakers give testimony at these meetings, telling of their own personal experiences. There are frequent testimonies of the receiving of the 'baptism of the Holy Ghost with signs following'. The meetings often end in ecstatic praise and ministry sessions. This movement now has chapters in many cities around the world, including several in London.

In the late 1950s there were stirrings among a number of Episcopal churchmen in the U.S.A. John and Joan Baker were a young Episcopal couple who 'had been searching for reality'. Their close friends, a dentist and his wife, experienced the 'baptism in the Holy Spirit' and such was the change in them that it prompted Joan Baker to ask the dentist's wife what had happened. The lady replied by speaking in tongues. Not long afterwards (after a short period of repentance) the Bakers, including a young daughter, were 'baptized in the Spirit' and spoke in tongues. They started to attend their local Episcopal church and testified of their experience to the vicar, Rev. Frank Maguire. He was impressed that they threw themselves whole-heartedly into parish work. The Bakers started to interest others in their experience. The vicar was concerned about the Bakers' influence in the church and consulted Dennis Bennett, the rector of a neighbouring church. In November 1959, after prayer with Joan Baker, Dennis Bennett claimed the experience of being 'filled with the Spirit' and spoke in tongues. Three days later Frank Maguire also spoke in tongues. Both these clergymen testified to a new freedom and success in witnessing, to the sick for whom they prayed being healed, and to an intense love for the Lord Jesus Christ and for fellow Christians.

Dennis Bennett started to send interested members of his congregation to the Bakers for counsel and a number of ministers as well as laymen claimed to be 'baptized in the Spirit'.[4]

Because of the growing number of people in his congregation who had had this experience and because of a rumour being spread about what was happening, Dennis told his parishioners of his experience at the morning service on Passion Sunday 1960. This disclosure caused confusion and anger in the congregation, though some were sympathetic. Shortly afterwards the Bennetts transferred to St Luke's, a small run-down mission church in Seattle. St Luke's has since grown and is held up as an example of the work of the Holy Spirit.[5]

In 1961 a magazine called *Trinity* was first published by the Blessed Trinity Society. This society was founded by Jean Stone, wife of a Lockhead Corporation executive, who had had a charismatic experience. This magazine has helped to spread the charismatic message through the denominations.[6] Later Mrs Stone divorced her husband and married the associate editor of the magazine.[7]

During the early 1960s a number of people in the Church of England and other old-established denominations had become dissatisfied with the quality of their own spiritual lives and with the state of the church. A number of clergymen (many of whom were Anglicans) were led into the charismatic experience. *Trinity* magazine played a part in a number of these experiences.[8] Some were encouraged to follow after the experience by an article by Dr Philip Hughes in the September 1962 issue of the *Churchman* magazine, telling of a visit he made to California at the invitation of Mrs Jean Stone.[9] Also significant were visits to Britain by David du Plessis[10] in 1960, Rev. Frank Maguire in 1963 and Larry Christensen[11] in the same year.[12]

The publication in 1962 of the sensational paperback book *The Cross and the Switchblade* by David Wilkerson gave considerable impetus to the growth of the movement. This book is an account of a country preacher's fight to help youngsters in the slums of New York. He moves among teenage gangsters and drug addicts. The book is written in the racy style of the modern novel (it was 'ghosted' by two well-known charismatic writers, John and Elizabeth Sherrill). The central character, David Wilkerson, is an Assemblies of God minister who is led by impressions and isolated verses of Scripture. He is clearly a very sincere man and the story is very moving. There is a chapter on the 'baptism of the Holy Spirit with the evidence of speaking in tongues', which undoubtedly influenced many readers to seek this experience for themselves. The book is very weak theologically and the Holy Spirit is exalted rather than the Lord Jesus. Several million copies of this work have been sold in many different languages. We shall come across the influence of this book again later on.

1964 saw the publication in *Crusade* magazine[13] of two articles by an Elim minister, Rev. Hywel Davies, on the growing charismatic renewal.[14]

Also in 1964 an interdenominational movement was founded which was destined to play a major role in the promotion of the charismatic movement — the Fountain Trust. This Trust, with its official magazine *Renewal*, saw itself as a prophetic voice within the church.[15]

A leading figure from the beginning of the movement in the United Kingdom has been the Anglican clergyman, Rev. Michael Harper. This one-time curate to John Stott at All Souls, Langham Place in London has since become a best-selling author. His books range from an account of the history of the charismatic phenomena (widely quoted in this work) to a number of books on the gifts themselves. Although he claims to have been an evangelical, he has since moved into a much more Catholic phase. He states in a book published in 1979, 'The Virgin Mary has come alive and I feel

I know her now, in the same way as my evangelical heritage helped me to know St Paul.'[16] But is the Christian exhorted to know Mary, or Paul for that matter? We are to know Christ and the power of his resurrection (Philippians 3:10).

The 1960s also saw the rise of the so-called 'Jesus movement' in the U.S.A. This sprang from the 'hippie' culture of the late 1950s and early 1960s and came as a result of the disillusionment with that form of drug culture. Its language was couched in hippie terms and exerted a wide influence over youngsters in the U.S.A. Many of the early 'Jesus people' groups were charismatic and either melted into more normal charismatic groups or became rabid heretical sects (e.g. the Children of God, of whom more in a moment), or faded away altogether.

The Fountain Trust, especially in the 1960s, organized many conferences and some of the speakers at these conferences were leading charismatics from the U.S.A.

By 1966—67 the Roman Catholic Church had begun to be interested in charismatic phenomena. This was partly due to the more open attitude to other denominations fostered by Pope John XXIII and the Second Vatican Council. During 1966, at Duquesne University in Pittsburgh, several lay Catholics started to meet for daily prayer. They had been influenced by the reading of David Wilkerson's book *The Cross and the Switchblade*. Some of them attended a Pentecostal house meeting, run by a woman, and had there the experience of 'the baptism and speaking in tongues'.[17] In March 1967 a meeting was organized at Notre Dame Roman Catholic University (U.S.A.). At this meeting seven people (all Roman Catholics) 'spoke in tongues'. This is regarded by many as the beginning of Catholic Pentecostalism.[18]

Demos Shakarian's influence on this movement was recognized by the Vatican in 1974 when he received 'an official appreciation of the role of the [FGBMFI] in reaching "millions" of Roman Catholic laymen.'[19]

This movement within Roman Catholicism grew rapidly and by the 1970s an annual 'renewal conference' was being held, with very large numbers attending. In 1976 the attendance topped 30,000.[20]

During the 1970s the charismatics began to organize and, as well as the established groups such as the Fountain Trust and the FGBMFI, a number of new groups came into existence. One which plays a major role was originally called 'Holy Spirit Teaching Ministries', which later became 'Christian Growth Ministries'. The leaders of this group are Derek Prince, Bob Mumford, Charles Simpson and Don Basham. Christian Growth Ministries is based in Fort Lauderdale, Florida, and publishes a magazine called *New Wine*, which has a worldwide circulation. Some of the Christian Growth Ministries' teaching has caused considerable controversy, particularly on the questions of water baptism and exorcism.[21] Don Basham and Derek Prince spread the 'deliverance ministry' throughout North America and this also had an impact in the United Kingdom. With some it became an unhealthy obsession. Any minor character defect or unusual happening was blamed on demon activity and great efforts were made to cast out demons or sometimes Satan himself.

1971 saw the first conference shared by Catholics and non-Catholics. This was the Fountain Trust conference held in Guildford. David Watson (then Rector of St Michael-le-Belfry, in York, a charismatic Anglican church) commented that he had been fearful about meeting Roman Catholics, but 'When we'd cleared away a lot of semantics I could not see any essential difference between what they believed and what I believed. On basics we were one in Christ though there might be some differences of opinion on secondary issues.'[22]

During 1975 the charismatic movement experienced another major controversy over the question of discipleship. The teaching in its most extreme form seems to have emanated from a charismatic group in Argentina. The chief spokesman for this group was an Argentinian, Juan Carlos Ortiz (though the group also consisted of a number of Western missionaries).

The teaching involved the loss of individuality and also the setting up of a hierarchy. Mr Ortiz said, 'What God wants is mashed potatoes. Not many potatoes — but one mashed potato. No potato can stand up and say, "Here am I: I'm a potato." The word must be *we*.'[23] The teaching on discipleship at the time also gave the impression that God could only speak to the individual through a chain of command. God spoke to the elder (or shepherd) and the shepherd spoke to the disciple. The impression has also been given that to safeguard against leaders abusing their position, they (the leaders or shepherds) must 'submit to Scripture as the final authority'.[24] But where does this leave the poor disciple? Has he no direct contact with his God, or is there no need for him to acknowledge the final authority of Scripture? In the U.S.A. there was for a time a split between two major groups over this question of discipleship, but at a conference held in 1977 differences were ironed out and a measure of unity established.

The charismatic movement is prone to this type of situation because they believe that revelation is progressive. The beginning of the movement in the 1960s saw the emphasis put on the actual experience of the 'baptism in the Spirit'. Then came the 'water baptism'[25] phase, to be followed by the period when exorcism was 'the thing'. Then came the 'discipleship' period and later still the emphasis was put on 'praise' (stemming largely from the writings of Merlin Carrothers).[26] Mr Carrothers taught that the Christian must learn to give praise to God in every circumstance of his/her life. This was taken to bizarre extremes (giving praise for divorce, etc.,) and spawned a new breed of 'praise' books. Once one part of the movement receives a 'revelation', that 'revelation' seems to work its way through the whole movement.

The 1970s seem to have been the age of the large inter-denominational conference, some held in ancient (and modern) English cathedrals, including Guildford (Church of England) and Westminster (Roman Catholic). At a conference held in 1976 in Jerusalem it was significant that delegates had to have interpreters and headphones to understand one another. The gift of 'tongues' and 'interpretation' is clearly limited in its application.

8.
The situation in the 1980's

As we come to the 1980s, we must acknowledge the difficulty of keeping up-to-date when the charismatic doctrine of progressive revelation means, by definition, that teachings rapidly lose their topicality and become dated. However, this chapter seeks to summarize some of the main developments in the first half of this decade.

The charismatic movement has settled down to a certain extent and has become accepted and respectable (though there are exceptions, as we shall see). Most of the denominations, especially in the U.S.A., have their own charismatic group or 'revival' fellowship. The modern movement started largely within the Anglican communion and has spread rapidly to Roman Catholic, Lutheran, Presbyterian, Congregational, Baptist, Brethren, Mennonite and Methodist churches and to many individuals who had no church affiliation.

It is disturbing to find that many who claim the experience of 'the baptism' are men with a liberal theology. Very few (though there are some) would claim to be fundamentalists. Evangelicalism is either misunderstood and/or treated as worse than heresy. Most staunch evangelicals would be considered 'beyond the pale' by many charismatics. The movement has tended to bring to the fore flamboyant, entertainer type ministers and to place no restraints on women preaching and teaching (in spite of Scripture). Indeed many leading figures in the movement are women, e.g. Jean Stone, Jean Darnell and a number of 'healers', including Agnes Sanford, Anne White and Ruth Carter Stapleton (sister of ex-U.S.

president Jimmy Carter). The most famous healing evangelist was undoubtedly Kathryn Kuhlmann.

There are a number of fringe groups who have been or are charismatic. The Children of God are perhaps the most obvious example of this. The sect started life under the leadership of one David Berg, who later changed his name to Moses. His message was fundamentalist/charismatic, but gradually the forces of evil drew him into a more and more extreme position. As the movement grew, Moses started to receive 'revelations' from 'angels' and 'spirits'. These revelations were taken down and published on the sect's own printing presses. They are known as 'Mo Letters'. These letters are said to be God's Word for today and have supplanted the Scriptures which are God's Word for yesterday.[1] Moses is also reported to have several concubines and his 'revelations' have included 'hookers[2] for Jesus' (girl followers willing to gain a convert to the sect by having sex with him) and child sex (a report in a prominent daily newspaper in 1981 stated that the movement was advocating that parents have sex with their own children).

There are numerous other small groups and sects, some respectable, some not. But by far the largest group after the denominational charismatics are the so called 'house churches'. In the United Kingdom there seem to be two main groups. One, which is countrywide, is associated with the names of Bryn Jones, Arthur Wallis, Dave Matthews, Ken Jones, Hugh Thomson and David Mansell. This group stresses that it is non-denominational. Its leaders, some of whom are named above, are called 'apostles' and 'prophets'. One church was formed when three smaller churches — a charismatic house group, an independent Pentecostal church and a Brethren assembly — amalgamated.[3] The group publishes a bi-monthly glossy magazine called *Restoration*.

The other group, which is smaller, seems to operate mainly around Essex and North-East London, though there are a few fellowships elsewhere. This group, too, has its own 'apostles'. They publish a magazine called *Fulness*. This group tends to be antinomian. They published some years ago a book on the Christian life entitled *Not Under Law*. Another work produced by the same author (one of the group's 'apostles') contained a very explicit chapter on positions for sexual intercourse which he recommended for married couples.

There is a certain amount of fellowship between the two groups and the occasional defection.

Also scattered around the country are independent house groups or those tied together by looser bonds than the highly organized groups mentioned. Some of these latter would not own the label 'charismatic', though they do believe in and practise 'the gifts of the Spirit'.

All these groups differ in theology — some being more biblical than others. Even the doctrines which they have in common, e.g. 'the baptism in the Spirit' and 'the gifts of the Spirit', are vastly different from one group to another. Some would teach that the baptism in the Spirit is a second experience, available for all who are truly born again; while others would teach that the baptism of the Spirit is new birth. The area of the gifts is an area where there is considerable difference of opinion.

The other great emphasis in the larger part of the movement is on the second coming of Jesus and most, though not all, would hold a premillennial position. Many see the 'restoration of the gifts' to the church as a sign that Jesus' return is imminent.

My observations in the last few years have revealed only one glimmer of hope within the movement. It is clear that some groups are being affected by Reformed theology; this has tended to persuade them to be more scriptural regarding the operation of the gifts and in some cases they have rejected the name 'charismatic' while still retaining the gifts.

Perhaps because of this tendency with some groups (how widespread this is, is difficult to ascertain) there seems to be a growing acceptance of charismatic practices among some evangelicals. While both parties acknowledge that there are differences in theology, they are prepared to co-operate in evangelism. There has been a shift towards the charismatics in the pages of the *Evangelical Times*, who have run a series of sympathetic articles by Peter Lewis. This has caused continued correspondence in the pages of this journal and, judging by the letters printed, honours are about even between those in sympathy with the movement and those opposed to it.

In the January 1982 issue of the *Evangelical Times* Rev. T. Omri Jenkins says, 'To my knowledge there is no real evidence of Holy Ghost power among [the charismatics]. In the light of Scripture and the history of the church I have to distinguish between the charismatic scene and true revival. The late Dr Lloyd-Jones told a number of us that many ministers had told him that they had received the baptism of the Holy Spirit and that he had made a point of asking each one whether he enjoyed new power in preaching the gospel. Sadly, they had all said "No." This in my view says it all.'

Jim Packer, the Anglican theologian, has also softened his attitude towards the charismatic movement. In an interview with the *Church of England Newspaper*, at about the time of the publication of his major work on the Holy Spirit *Keep in Step with the Spirit*,[4] he said, 'All [the charismatics] seemed to offer [twenty years ago] was unscriptural Spirit-baptism and unedifying tongue-speaking. Since then I've experienced mostly good among charismatics . . .'

Within the movement there is still the desire for large gatherings and all the different groups within the movement appear to have their own conferences. There are the Dales Bible Week (held at Harrogate) and the Downs Bible Week (held in the South). These conferences cater for a large number of people (Dales 10,000; Downs 3,000) in the Harvestime/Restoration circle). Gerald Coates organizes the Kingdom Life conferences for those who belong to his circle and the Chard group of fellowships have their own Rivers of Life conferences. There are a number of other annual gatherings of a charismatic flavour, perhaps the most famous being 'Greenbelt'. This is largely taken up with rock, pop and folk music. A number of one-off gatherings also occur. For example, over the May 1982 Bank Holiday weekend there was a gathering held at Wembley arena. Called 'The Banquet' it was billed as 'a feast of Rock and Praise'. There were rock bands, singers, a choir and a drama group. The speakers were David Pawson, David Watson and Gerald Coates.

The movement is reported to be widely influential among Anglicans. On an *Everyman* programme broadcast on BBC1 on 2 March 1982 it was stated that half the parishes in the country had been influenced by the charismatic movement. This shows the amazing extent of the movement within the established church.

On the house-church front David Pawson is reported as saying that there are '100,000 house groups averaging ten adults each meeting regularly in Britain'.[5]

A number of charismatic groups in the U.S.A. are stock-piling weapons and are engaging in combat training so that they can defend themselves when the persecution which they expect starts. At least one group has reacted violently against the forces of law and order. A number of people were killed.[6]

Perhaps the most serious trend within the movement is the undermining of the historical and biblical evangelical view. Several of the movement's well-known preachers say that Christians should not be engaging in evangelism. We need prophets first, because a prophetic ministry precedes an evangelical ministry. Did not John the Baptist (a prophet) precede the Lord Jesus Christ (who came to preach the gospel)? Can it be, one wonders, that men like Spurgeon (and many, many others) got it all wrong? Yet this is what David Pawson and George Tarletan (and maybe others) are saying.

Then there is the strange phenomenon of a return to Jewish festivals. David Pawson advocates that Gentiles ought to be going to Jerusalem to observe the Feast of Tabernacles. He quotes Zechariah 14:16 where it says, 'The survivors from all the nations that have attacked Jerusalem will go up year after year to worship the King, the Lord Almighty, and to celebrate the Feast of Tabernacles. If any of the peoples of the earth do not go up to Jerusalem to worship the King, the Lord Almighty, they will have no rain.' He suggests, indeed states quite clearly, that this is the reason why the United Kingdom and the United States of America have had no rain. When this message was recorded is not clear, but there has been no prolonged period of drought in either country in the early 1980s!

One wonders if Mr Pawson really expects to be taken seriously, yet there are no voices, that I am aware of, raised against this Judaizing trend.

There is also a book published in the U.S.A. that advocates celebrating Jewish festivals in churches and homes.[7] It is 'not obligatory', but the book gives all the equipment needed to celebrate each feast in the appropriate Jewish manner. There are certainly great dangers in what is already being said and one fears where this Judaizing trend could ultimately lead. No wonder Jews in Israel (and elsewhere) are rejoicing that Christians are joining them in celebrating the Feast of Tabernacles. But the Christians who do celebrate the feasts are losing their distinctiveness as Christians and going back to something that has been fulfilled in Christ. Surely the whole tenor of New Testament teaching is that the need for sacrifices and festivals to remember historical events is now done away in Christ. Our God has shed forth the Holy Spirit upon us and we may worship alone or together in fellowship with others. We do not need, as the Jews of old, to go up to Jerusalem to worship before the ark. We have an ark within, where the spiritual law is (symbolized by the stone tablets), where the resurrection life is (symbolized by Aaron's rod), where Christ the Bread of heaven dwells (symbolized by the pot of manna). We do not need to go to Jerusalem; we worship our Father and his Son the Lord Jesus in Spirit and in truth.

There are growing differences of opinion in the charismatic movement. Michael Harper, a leader among Anglican charismatics and editor of *Renewal Magazine*, said in *Today* in March 1984 that 'The church must go on having renewals or revivals, but without splitting into renewed and unrenewed members.' This is, of course, exactly what did happen in the early days of the movement. The tendency has always been for the charismatic element in a church, even if in a minority, to impose its will on the rest. Mr Harper is clearly committed to the charismatic cause within the established denominations, but particularly within the Church of England. Other charismatic teachers seem to take an opposite view. Gerald Coates, for example, said in *Today* in May 1983, 'I am convinced that the church system is utterly corrupt.' There is clearly disagreement, too, over the question of modern-day 'prophets' and 'apostles'. Michael Harper said in *Today* in March 1984, 'I don't think that the *office* of prophet or apostle still exists.' Gerald Coates is clearly committed to the view that they *do* exist.[8]

Another recent publication is that of a book by the late Dr Martin Lloyd-Jones, *Joy Unspeakable*, which shows very well that he believed in a 'second experience' after conversion, a 'baptism with the Holy Spirit'. This will, no doubt, give charismatics hope that they are winning the battle against die-hard evangelicalism.

The movement continues to throw up its share of eccentricities. In 1983 a book was published in the United Kingdom entitled *Exodus II*, by Steve Lightle. This book claimed that God is preparing another exodus for the Jews, this time guiding them by 'visions', 'visits from angels', etc., to prepare for this exodus. He is quite convinced, like many charismatics, that the Jews are still God's chosen people, whether they believe in him or not. (This is a vast area of discussion which I cannot touch on here.) The book quotes many scriptures to prove the point of the visions and other experiences, but Mr Lightle seems to have little sense of history and of prophecy being fulfilled in the past. He, like many in the movement, seems to believe that all the prophecies of the Bible will find their fulfilment in these 'last days'.

One example which he gives of fulfilled prophecy is really quite funny. He says, 'We read in Isaiah 27:6, "In the days to come Jacob will take root, Israel will blossom and sprout; and they will fill the whole world with fruit." Wherever I have gone in Europe I have had the opportunity to eat "Jaffa oranges". The Bible promised us that "the fruit of Israel will fill the whole earth". It is happening today.'[9] It is just such a failure to distinguish between a physical fulfilment of prophecy and spiritual fulfilment that has already caused so much confusion.

In the January/February 1985 issue of *Restoration* magazine the editor, David Matthew, tells of a woman in her sixties who was 'baptized in the Holy Spirit'. When someone asked her to describe the experience she said, 'Ooh, it was wonderful! . . . It was like . . . er . . . like . . . like taking my corsets off!' This sums up so much about the charismatic attitude to God: not a growing reverence and awe, but a growing light-heartedness and over-familiarity with the great and awesome and holy God who created the universe.

Let us never lose a sense of awe as we come before a holy God and let us pray that the one whom the charismatic would claim to have an experience of, the Holy Spirit, will be poured out in a true revival which will show us all what God is really like.

9.
Summary of historical section

It is very obvious from this historical review that after the period of the use of gifts and miracles in the New Testament, most other manifestations have been in heretical groups. Even the Quakers cannot truly be regarded as evangelical, due to their unbiblical doctrines. They believed in sinless perfection (Fox said that he had grown up into perfection[1]) and also so spiritualized baptism and the Lord's Supper as to do away with them altogether.

Wesley, though he appears to have been in favour of the gifts, was not so happy when actually faced with charismatic phenomena in his own societies. He also condemned the French Prophets.

It is only in recent times that these phenomena have started to take place among groups of people who could be described as evangelical Christians. The overwhelming impression, when we study these phenomena and the groups within which they are practised, is that they are not Christian phenomena. They take place among heretical groups and many non-Christian religions and even among people of no religion at all.

Part II   The teachings

10.
Charismatics and the Bible

In our assessment of the modern charismatic movement we must now turn our attention to their teaching.

The most serious and fundamental of the errors into which the movement has fallen, an error which leads to so many more false ideas, is in their attitude to the Bible. Most charismatics would pay lip-service to the evangelical view that Scripture is the infallible and authoritative Word of God. However, they would not claim that it is sufficient.

The early Quakers took the view that there were certain books of the Bible which were missing from the canon. They believed that certain Apocryphal books were inspired, such as Clement's Epistle, The Reply of Jesus to Abgar King of Edessa and the Book of Enoch. They sometimes quoted from these more obscure books. For example, the followers of James Naylor[1] quoted from the 'Epistle from Lentulus to the Roman Senate' to prove that Naylor *looked* like Jesus.[2]

Fisher, an early Friend, sums up the Quaker position by saying, 'Who was it that said to the Spirit of God, O Spirit, blow no more, inspire no more men, make no more prophets from Ezra's day and downwards till Christ, and from John's day downwards forever?'[3] This is a question that could have been uttered by a charismatic in our day.

At least one present-day teacher has taken a similar stance stating, 'We know from internal evidence that the Bible is incomplete. There are at least three letters of Paul's missing, beside some works by prophets of the Old Testament.[4] Mr North does go on to say that the Bible is 'perfect enough

71

for God's purposes . . . among men in this age'. Perhaps one of the books of the Old Testament that he believes is missing is the Book of Enoch, which in fact is now available.[5] The evangelical view is that the Scriptures are complete. All the books God meant us to have have survived in the canon. A more widely known charismatic teacher, Catherine Marshall, says in her book *Something More* (in her explanation of John 16:13), 'In fact, it seemed to me that Jesus' promise of "further truth" gives us clear reasons to believe that not all the truth and instruction Christ has to give us is contained in the canon of the Old and New Testaments. How could it be? He who is Truth will never find the people of any century able to receive everything he wants to give.'[6] This seems to sum up the fundamental problem of the movement and to be an extremely dangerous attitude. It opens the movement up to all sorts of extra-biblical revelations. How does one argue with anyone who claims to be directly speaking God's message, whether in prophecy, tongues or explanations of a vision?

Most charismatics today would deny that prophecies and other messages should be placed alongside Scripture, but the danger is there nevertheless. The Children of God, mentioned earlier, are an extreme example, but nonetheless illustrate that it is possible for charismatics to reach a position where what comes to a leader by way of 'revelation' replaces the Bible: 'The Bible is God's Word for yesterday, the Mo Letters are God's Word for today.'

Michael Buss has said, 'If such prophecies [as are given in the charismatic movement] were written down (and not infrequently they are!) no amount of argument can avoid recognizing that the document would immediately be the *written* word of God. Such is the dimension of the modern charismatic movement that we could in fact collect a vast quantity of written material purporting to be records of the directly spoken, naked words of God, in English! The material would, we are sure, be a strange hotch-potch of scriptural   exhortations,   non-scriptural   notions   and circumstantial directives to groups or individuals. It would also contain predictions of events yet future. We would call it the "Charismatic's Bible", for it would be a marvellous record of extra-biblical revelation, infallible and authoritative. We simply cannot avoid this conclusion — though I suspect most charismatics would beat a hasty retreat from it! It is ruled totally invalid according to the fulness and sufficiency of the only truly inspired book, the Bible.'[7]

A well-known charismatic leader from the U.S.A., J. Rodman Williams, speaking of present-day prophecy, has stated, 'In prophecy, God speaks. It is as simple and profound and startling as that! What happens in the fellowship is that the word may suddenly be spoken by anyone present, and so variously, a "Thus saith the Lord" breaks forth in the fellowship.'[8]

In an issue of the magazine *Logos* published in 1977 Williams explains, 'I do not intend in any way to place contemporary experience on the same level of authority as the Bible. Rather do I vigorously affirm the decisive authority of Scripture, hence, God does not speak just as authoritatively today as he spoke to the biblical authors. *But he does continue to speak* [he did not stop with the close of the New Testament canon] ; thus, he "moves through and beyond the records of past witness"; for he is the living God who still speaks and acts among his people.'[9]

This seems a view perilously close to that of the Children of God leader, David Berg, and certainly leaves a very wide loophole for the weaker brother or sister. Rodman Williams and Mrs Marshall clearly believe in progressive revelation. If we take this view we have no sure foundation left. When did God stop speaking in an authoritative way and start speaking in a less authoritative way? Anyone can claim (and indeed many do) a direct revelation from God in prophecy, tongues or vision. Sometimes these 'revelations' are quite scriptural. Often, however, they are clearly unscriptural (see Children of God earlier). All down the ages, as we have seen in the historical review, men and women have made 'a message from God' the excuse for exaggerated or immoral behaviour. Unfortunately today's movement is no different.

Because of this 'God has spoken to me and through me' attitude, many charismatic leaders, preachers and writers have an exalted view of their own ministry. For example, David du Plessis tells us in the introduction to his book *The Spirit Bade Me Go*: 'This book really "just happened". Most of the material comes from talks and lectures given without script or notes as the Holy Spirit gave or manifested the Word. [Yes!, that's right "the Word"!] They were "revelations I received from Him".'[10] We can see Michael Buss's proposition in action — the book *The Spirit Bade Me Go* is 'the Word of God'. We have Mr du Plessis's word on it!

A number of charismatic preachers and 'prophets' believe that as they open their mouths the Word of God is spoken, or that God will reveal to their minds a sentence or two and, as that is spoken, so God reveals more until the message is complete.

The way prophecy came to the Old Testament prophets was rather different. They didn't stand before God's people hardly knowing what to say. God revealed his message to them by word or vision in private and then the prophet went and proclaimed it. (See, for example, Exodus 3 and 4; Isaiah 1:1; 2:1; 6 (verses 9, 10 in particular); 7:3, 4; Jeremiah 1; 2:1; Ezekiel 1:3; 2:1–3). In this sense Old Testament prophecy is more comparable to present-day preaching, for the preacher receives his message in private and then proclaims it before the people.

The key to our understanding of present-day revelation is, it seems to me, Hebrews 1:1, 2. God spoke to the fathers through the prophets; in contrast, now, in these last days, God has spoken through his Son, Jesus Christ. There is no greater revelation that God will make to mankind, for Jesus is the culmination, the climax of all revelation. Nothing, surely, can be added to him. The Bible is the record of what *he* said, what his own personal followers wrote, eyewitness accounts (e.g. the 'apostles' doctrine' of Acts 2:42) in written form. To look for further revelation on top of the climax of God's revelation seems blasphemous. Like Philip in John 14: 7–10, the charismatic is not satisfied with Jesus. He seems to wish to turn away from Jesus and pursue some further revelation. But the work of the Holy Spirit, whom the charismatic seeks to follow, 'will not speak on his own' or give some new revelation, 'he will bring glory to me [Jesus] by taking from what is mine and making it known to you' (John 16:13–14).[11]

The charismatic believes that the Old Testament prophets had a greater revelation of God than Christians today, but the New Testament seems to indicate that this is not true (see, for example, 2 Corinthians 3 and 4).

The Scriptures themselves have also been endowed with the power to bring salvation, for Paul says to Timothy that 'The holy Scriptures' (and he means primarily the Old Testament) 'are able to make you wise for salvation through faith in Christ Jesus' (2 Timothy 3:15).

Sometimes the charismatic movement of today is referred to as 'the charismatic revival'. But it bears little resemblance to any revival of the past. 'Revival' is sometimes used in the American sense as a meeting or series of meetings aimed at increasing the zeal of Christians or of increasing the number of church members. But this is not revival in the classic sense. Duncan Campbell's definition of revival was that it was when the Spirit of God moved upon a whole community. The 'charismatic revival' fails to fulfil the second definition, though it might fulfil the first. We shall discuss this topic more fully later.

During revivals of past ages, converts have been hungry to hear the Word of God expounded as well as to read it privately. An entry from the diary of Archibald Alexander (1772–1851) during a time of revival around the year 1791 states, 'I preached . . . to a small congregation. In the time of sermon, the people appeared to be impressed, and to drink in the Word with greediness. I therefore continued my discourse for nearly two hours, and then dismissed the congregation.

I sat in the pulpit for fifteen minutes, but no person offered to go away. After some time I arose and told the people, that as they were not disposed to leave the House of God, their meditations might be assisted by the singing of a hymn; after which I again spoke about three-quarters of an hour. There were few individuals in the House who did not appear deeply affected.'[12]

In the biography of the great revival preacher, Duncan Campbell, we read that during the Hebrides revival, 'Hunger for the Word of God was so great that when the service finished in the small hours of the morning, the people assembled again a short distance away in the police station, where many found the Saviour.'[13]

Oh, that the Spirit of God would give similar hunger for his Word in the charismatic movement! Instead we see that the Bible is neglected (and often not even referred to), it is misunderstood (the whole movement is based on misunderstood Scripture) and preaching is despised.

11.
The gifts in the charismatic movement

In a general review of the gifts as manifested in the modern movement, we will rapidly gain an impression of considerable confusion. One teacher claims one thing and another will claim something different and it is clear that both cannot be correct. When all is said and done, it is abundantly clear that personal experience decides the issue, and not the Scriptures; and when people give precedence to experience their interpretation of Scripture is coloured or distorted by their experience.

The present work will not be an attempt to duplicate the work of biblical scholars such as Robert Gromacki and George Gardiner, but will be limited to comments on just some of the 'gifts'.

Healing

Many in the charismatic movement today claim that God is performing healing miracles through the church, as he was through the Lord Jesus Christ when he was upon earth. Some claim that the greater works mentioned by Jesus in John 14:12 are those miracles and healings being performed today.

Is there documentary proof that people are being healed of otherwise incurable diseases? There are many claims that cancer and other organic diseases are being healed. But can these claims be substantiated?

Some years ago the leg-lengthening ministry was popularized. It is a well-known fact that many people have one leg slightly shorter than the other. This sometimes accounts for some spinal troubles, but with most of us it is so slight that no one would ever notice it. There were 'healers' going round laying hands on people and causing the shorter leg to grow to match the longer. Many people claim to have seen a leg grow before their eyes. I personally heard testimony of this type of healing. However, after a short time it was 'revealed' that the man performing these miracles was not quite right spiritually. The leg-lengthening healer was admonished in some way, departed the scene and eventually this type of ministry went out of fashion.

Crusade magazine published an article a few years ago containing the testimony of someone who had seen people in South America 'receive' gold fillings in their teeth, with a cross stamped in the filling — perhaps a sort of heavenly hallmark! John MacArthur tells of a woman who wrote to him saying that she had received a new 'belly-button'.[1]

One of the most famous and popular healers was the late Kathryn Kuhlmann. Several books of her miracles and some three biographies are available to the public. There is no doubt at all that this lady had a very extraordinary 'ministry' and made a lasting impression on many who met or saw her. Her approach to healing was somewhat different from that of most charismatic healers. She did not have queues of people streaming forward for hands to be laid on them, but as she spoke people were 'healed' spontaneously all over the building. Miss Kuhlmann laid great emphasis on the fact that it was the Holy Spirit who healed, not Miss Kuhlmann. As a physician pointed out, 'If the patient doesn't improve, the Holy Spirit, not Kathryn Kuhlmann gets the blame.'[2] This same physician, a Dr Nolan, investigated twenty-three cases of healing (the names and addresses being supplied by Miss Kuhlmann). His conclusion was that not one of these 'miracles' was genuine.[3]

John MacArthur quotes the story of the man whose wife had been 'healed' of cancer. Mr MacArthur asked the man, 'How is she now?'

'Oh, she is dead,' said the man.

'She died? How long after the healing?'

He replied, 'One year.'[4]

What a sad sort of healing this is!

People who go to healing meetings and are not healed are often castigated for their lack of faith. This is a common occurrence and causes mental suffering to those who are already suffering physically.

There seems no doubt that those suffering from diseases in which a perfectly normal organ doesn't function properly are helped and maybe even cured by these 'healers'. But they are also often helped by medical doctors and, we might add, by spiritualist healers and others.

'Search the literature as I have,' writes Dr Nolan, 'and you will find no documented cures by healers of gallstones, heart disease, cancer, or any other serious organic disease. Certainly you'll find patients temporarily relieved of their upset stomachs, their chest pains, their breathing problems; and you will find healers, and believers, who will interpret this interruption of symptoms as evidence that the disease is cured. But when you track the patient down and find out what happened later, you will always find the "cure" to have been purely symptomatic and transient. The underlying disease remains.'[5]

Do these 'healers' operate in the same way as Jesus did when he was on the earth? The answer must be a resounding 'No!' The 'healings' of the charismatic movement take place generally in meetings and are often the result of whipped-up emotions. Jesus healed in large gatherings (though not with choirs and entertainment), but many of his healings took place in the streets and roads of Palestine as he was travelling. The widow of Nain's son (Luke 7:11–17), the centurion's servant (Matthew 8:5–13; Luke 7:1–10), the woman with the haemorrhage (Luke 8:43–48), the Gadarene demoniac (Luke 8:26–39), blind men (Luke 18:35–43; John 9:1–11) and lepers (Luke 5:12–16; Luke 17:11–19) were all healed in the streets and fields as Jesus travelled around Galilee and Judea.

There is no record in the literature of the charismatic movement, that I am aware of, which has dared to claim that healers today are performing this kind of miracle. How often have I, and many others, longed to minister healing to a person in a wheelchair or to a crippled child in the street! But these things do not happen.

If half the people claiming to be healers were genuine and went round the hospital wards of our land, the problems of the National Health Service would be solved almost overnight. Instead, so-called healers create havoc wherever they go, bringing people in to expect healing and hardening people's hearts against the gospel when the 'healings' fail. The most important thing to bear in mind is that the Lord's name is brought into disrepute.

Prophecy

The 'gift of prophecy' is widely used in the present-day movement. It comes in many different forms, from an utterance in contemporary English to the explanation of a 'vision'.

Normally the gift is expected to come in the course of a meeting, when a prophet will be inspired to utter a prophecy. Very often these prophecies are nothing more than watered-down, modernized and sometimes inaccurately quoted scriptural exhortations. It is usually obvious by the wording of the prophecy which version of the Bible is favoured by the prophet. In the early 1960s it was mostly the Authorized Version; now it is more likely to be New American Standard (or even Good News), which is widely favoured. These prophecies may be long or short, understandable or almost unintelligible, fairly scriptural or downright heretical. In fourteen years in the charismatic movement I *never* heard a word of prophecy disagreed with. All seem to be accepted as a 'direct word from the Lord'. If anyone does disagree, he never says so.

Some prophecies will claim to foretell the future. In the

1960s, for example, a number of prophecies and visions were given, foretelling a revival which would sweep through the Medway Towns. The revival would start in Walderslade (which is at the head of a valley) and flow down the valley, as lava flows down from a volcano, into Chatham and out to Gillingham and Rochester. Though St Mark's, Gillingham,[6] was then at the height of its ministry, under Rev. John Collins, and though smaller groups were dotted about the Medway Towns, this prophecy has yet to be fulfilled.

Another prophecy published in *Renewal* magazine in April 1973 stated, 'My children, know that I am with you in everything you do. When you feel inadequate and unable to meet the task I have set before you, then look to me and I will supply the needed strength. When you learn to recognize where your strength lies then you will discover the secret of working for Me and with Me. I am your strength, your joy, your peace, your hope. Without Me, nothing you do will ever last eternally. My power working through you will bring to nought the things of time, and establish eternal values within your being.

'In the coming months I will sweep through the land by My power. The people of the North will see it and be glad, and those in the South shall awaken to the moving of My Spirit with renewed joy. I am making war on principalities and powers and it is My desire to use you in My plan so that all the works of Satan shall be destroyed by the anointing that abides upon you. As you become obedient to My commands and follow the way I am opening up to you, so shall the mountains fall flat before you. In the coming days you shall see such a sweep of My power that will not be explained by natural means. People will be changed before your eyes, and you will see the power that I can use when I have yielded vessels before Me. Praise Me with all your heart for this is the day of joy. Do not be sad, My children, but lift your hearts and voices in song. The Lord is about to do great things in your land. Believe Me, and nothing shall be impossible unto you.'[7]

This prophecy, which is so typical of many given in the movement, is a strange mixture of scriptural-sounding exhortation and wishful thinking. As anyone will know, there was and is *no revival* in North or South to fulfil this prophecy. The Lord did *not* 'sweep through the land'. Can any serious charismatic or Pentecostal claim that this prophecy was fulfilled? He must in all honesty admit that it wasn't! Therefore it is by scriptural definition a false prophecy and the person who gave it is (sad to say) a false prophet (cf. Deuteronomy 18:21,22). Unfortunately many charismatics would claim that it *was* fulfilled in the growing charismatic movement. This 'charismatic revival', as we have already seen, does not match up with a true definition of revival.

We could quote many more false prophecies that have come from the movement. But perhaps the examples already quoted suffice to show that what is claimed as prophecy is no such thing. Many are led astray, discouraged and disappointed when these prophecies are not fulfilled.

Tongues

By far the most controversial area of the charismatic movement's claims is in the area of speaking in tongues. Indeed, the movement is often dubbed 'the tongues movement' though the charismatic claims that *all* the New Testament gifts are being manifested in the movement.

Definitions of tongues by various Pentecostal and charismatic speakers and writers vary considerably. Oral Roberts says, 'The gift of tongues was spoken to God on behalf of other believers, searching out inner weaknesses and needs, and linking them with the will of God and with the mind of the Spirit for them. The gift of interpretation gives God's response to the Spirit's intercession.'[8]

Stanley H. Frodsham, a Pentecostal, says, 'The child of God is privileged to have speech with God and no man understands this secret speech, for the saint is allowed to speak in the language of divinity — a language unknown to humanity . . . The humblest saint can enjoy supernatural converse with Him who made the worlds, in a language not understood by man, or by the devil either.'[9]

Larry Christenson believes that the gift is to be used in worship and adoration.[10]

Some interpret tongues as a gift to be used in preaching to people who do not clearly understand one's native language or as a sign to an unbeliever. There are stories of charismatics who have been in hospital and who have felt led to speak in tongues. In the next bed has been an Indian or Pakistani Muslim who has testified to hearing the tongues-speaker preaching the gospel in an Indian or Pakistani dialect. Others claim that the 'groans that words cannot express' of Romans 8:26 are tongues used in intercession. From these few examples we can see that the Pentecostal and charismatic movements display some confusion over this gift.

Reading the Acts of the Apostles (2:1—13), we see very clearly that the tongues spoken were real languages, for the Jews gathered in Jerusalem for the feast said that they could understand what the disciples were saying. We even have a list of the languages used (vv. 9—11). Now these men did not *need* to be spoken to in the languages of the countries and districts they came from, for they all spoke at least one (and probably more) language in common, i.e., Hebrew. So the sign of tongues must have fulfilled another purpose. In 1 Corinthians 14:20—23 we are informed that tongues are a sign to unbelievers (v. 22). The unbelievers were the Jews. We can figure this out from verse 21, following it back to its source in the Old Testament in Isaiah 28:11,12. By studying all the cases of the occurrence of 'tongues' in the Acts, we can see that Jews were present at each event. No doubt the significance of the gift did not escape the understanding of those Jews who heard it. (For a fuller and better treatment of this subject readers are encouraged to obtain the excellent book by George Gardiner, *The Corinthian Catastrophe*).[11]

This particular gift should be quite easy to test, as indeed are healing and prophecy. The modern tape-recorder means that we can record 'tongues' and analyse them to find out whether they are genuine languages or not. This has been done by a number of linguists over the years. A psychologist, Robert L. Dean, and William Welmes (Professor of African Languages at U.C.L.A.) are among those who have carried out this type of research. Professor Welmes described the modern phenomenon as 'a linguistic fraud and monstrosity'.[12]

David Christie-Murray says in his book, 'The witness of linguistic scholars is unanimously against the claims that genuine languages are spoken . . . Henke records that in hearing a hundred or more people speaking in tongues at Chicago revival meetings, he heard no one speak in any of the six languages he knew.'[13]

Dr W. J. Samarin (Professor of Linguistics at the University of Toronto), who has written several books dealing with this subject, says, 'A person hearing or thinking he heard Swahili words would tend to "hear" a lot more Swahili.' Dr Samarin, who has researched long and hard on tongues says this, 'Over a period of five years I have taken part in meetings in Italy, Holland, Jamaica, Canada and the United States. I have observed old-fashioned Pentecostals and neo-Pentecostals. I have been in small meetings in private houses as well as in mammoth public meetings. I have seen such different cultural settings as are found among the Puerto Ricans of the Bronx, the snake-handlers of the Appalachians and the Russian Molakans of Los Angeles . . . I have interviewed tongue-speakers and tape-recorded and analysed countless samples of tongues. In every case, glossolalia[14] turns out to be linguistic nonsense. In spite of superficial similarities, glossolalia is fundamentally not language.'[15]

Dr John P. Kildahl, a psychotherapist, conducted a study of tongues over a period of years. He writes, 'Linguistic scholars work with precise definitions of what constitutes a natural human language. Glossolalia fails to meet the criteria of these definitions. Specifically, the work of Charles F.

Hockett details sixteen criteria for language. The research of linguists clearly reveals that the spoken utterances of glossolalists do not meet these criteria.'[16]

Charismatics would no doubt say that some of these men are unbelievers and therefore are judging a spiritual gift by non-spiritual standards. Many would say that the languages are not necessarily human languages anyway, but may well be angelic (cf. 1 Corinthians 13:1), but angels, too, must have grammar and language structure. Donald Gee, a well-known Pentecostal, says that interpretation of tongues was 'quite capable of being tested by anybody who might happen to have a naturally acquired knowledge of the tongue spoken'.[17] A language does not become a non-language just because the person listening to it is an unbeliever.

It is very clear that there is tremendous psychological pressure put on many people in charismatic circles to speak in tongues. There are exhortations to 'enter into the gift' and often there is a period of 'free worship', which consists of the whole group speaking or singing in tongues at the same time. If one or two people in a meeting are not speaking in tongues, although no-one may actually say anything directly to them, they are under enormous pressure to let go of their restraints and gabble along with the rest.

Dr Kildahl tells of a typical group gathered around the altar rail of a church. Several prayed in English and one individual, Bill, prayed to receive the Spirit. The guest preacher began to speak in tongues. Bill remembered feeling as if there was 'an electrifying charge in the air'. The leader asked if any desired to speak in tongues. Several said that they did. 'They knelt at the altar as a group, and the leader encouraged them to try to "receive" this ability. He went from one to another, laying his hands on each person's head. Bill told me that with a prayer in tongues and with encouragement, the leader asked him to make an effort to move his lips in a free and relaxed manner. "Say after me what I say, and then go on speaking in the tongue that the Lord will give you." "Aish nay gum nay tayo . . ." prayed the leader and waited for

Bill to repeat the same sounds and then to go on in his own
words. Bill tried, "Aish nay gum nay tayo . . ." and then
stopped. "Aish nay gum nay tayo . . . Aish nay gum nay
tayo . . ." The leader, keeping both hands on Bill's head
again prayed that Bill would open himself to receive the
"gift of the Spirit".' After a few more repetitions of the
same phrase Bill said, 'Aish nay gum . . . aish nay . . . anna
gayna . . . ayna gamma keena . . . kayna geena anna naymanna
naymanna.'[18]

Many instances of tongues and the introduction of the
experience into someone's life are very similar to this incident. In other words, our conclusion is that tongues can be
taught and are a mental/psychological manifestation rather
than purely spiritual and spontaneous, as the charismatic
suggests.

Dr Kildahl also quotes an instance of someone offering
to move another person's chin while he repeated certain
phrases in a tongue. Inevitably the person ended up speaking
in tongues and was overjoyed by the experience.[19]

A great deal of this tongues-teaching goes on. This is
in some respects surprising, as the gift is supposed to be
spontaneous and spiritual. But it does prove that, one way
or another, if someone wants an experience, he or she is
prepared to do almost anything to obtain it. When you give
someone a present, they simply receive it; they do not have
to be taught to receive it.

Larry Christensen says that to speak in tongues you have
to '. . . lapse into silence and resolve to speak not a syllable
of any language you have ever learned. Your thoughts are
focused on Christ, and then you simply lift up your voice
and speak out confidently in the faith that the Lord will
take the sound you give to Him, and shape it into a
language.'[20]

Harold Bredesen says that seekers should 'try to visualize
Jesus as a person . . . to yield their voices and organs of speech
to the Holy Spirit . . . [and] repeat certain elementary
sounds . . . such as "bah – bah – bah" or something similar'.[21]

These examples would be quite laughable if they were not so serious and they are, of course, without any scriptural foundation.

Interpretation

This gift stands or falls with tongues and/or prophecy. It is easily tested, like tongues.

Dr Kildahl quotes the case of a young man, the son of missionary parents, who had been raised in Africa. This young man attended a meeting where he was a complete stranger. He rose and repeated the Lord's prayer in the African dialect he had learned as a child. The interpretation offered was of the imminence of the second coming of the Lord Jesus.[22]

Another incident quoted by John F. Walvoord in his book on the Holy Spirit tells of 'a young seminarian who memorized a Psalm in Hebrew. At a tongues meeting he stood to his feet and pretended to be speaking in tongues as he recited the Psalm. After he had finished, the interpreter woefully failed in translating what had been spoken.'[23]

12.
The cessation of New Testament gifts

We now have to consider why the New Testament gifts were given and to see from Scripture whether we should expect these gifts to be manifested (a) throughout the church age, or (b) in the latter days – in other words, can and should we expect to see the gifts of the Spirit manifested in the same way as in the Acts of the Apostles and 1 Corinthians?

We have already learned from our historical survey that Chrysostom (345–407) and Augustine (354–430) had not seen and did not expect to see the gifts operating in the church. It was Chrysostom who said, 'This whole place (i.e. 1 Corinthians 12) is very obscure, but the obscurity is produced by our ignorance of the facts referred to and by their cessation, being such as then used to occur but now no longer take place.'[1]

Why were the miraculous gifts bestowed upon the early church and did everyone exercise miraculous gifts? Hebrews 2:3,4 tells us that 'signs, wonders and various miracles and gifts of the Holy Ghost' were confirmation that the ministry of the Lord Jesus was of God. God was testifying that his Son was who he claimed to be.

These signs and wonders were also confirmation of an apostle's ministry (see 2 Corinthians 12:12). Here Paul is defending his own ministry and he says, 'The things that mark an apostle – signs, wonders and miracles – were done among you with great perseverance.' It is clear that signs, wonders and miracles were the outward signs or badge of an apostle's ministry. They were not, even in those early times of the church, the prerogative of every Christian — otherwise Paul would not have been able to claim them as a mark of his apostleship (see also Romans 15:15–19).

It is plain that gifts were manifested in the Corinthian church, but Paul says, 'To one there is given through the Spirit the message of wisdom, to another the message of knowledge by means of the same Spirit, to another faith by the same Spirit . . .' (1 Corinthians 12:8,9). This would indicate that *one* person was given *one* gift, whereas an apostle was able to use several or all the gifts.

The fact that the miraculous gifts were manifested in the Corinthian church was no doubt a confirmation of the apostle's ministry and it is very clear that the gifts operated less frequently as the church grew in maturity. One only has to read through the Acts of the Apostles to see that signs and wonders became progressively less frequent as we go through the book. John MacArthur tells us that the last recorded miracle was recorded in A.D. 58 (Acts 28:7–10).[2] Miraculous gifts (including tongues) are mentioned in 1 Corinthians, but are not mentioned at all in the later epistles. Is it likely that something so important would not be mentioned by the other apostolic writers — John, Peter, James, Jude, the writer of the Epistle to the Hebrews and the Gospel writers? (The only Gospel to mention miraculous signs being performed by ordinary believers is Mark 16:15–18. Even here the charismatic will be hard pressed to prove that all these signs are in operation today — for example, snake-handling and poison-drinking. There is a Pentecostal sect in the U.S.A. which does go in for snake-handling and frequently people, believers, are bitten and die. But this is by no means normal practice among Pentecostal/charismatic groups and indeed is frowned upon by 'respectable' Pentecostals.)

Pentecostals and charismatics both resort to Joel 2:23: 'Be glad, O people of Zion, rejoice in the Lord your God, for he has given you in righteousness the autumn rains. He sends you abundant showers, both autumn and spring rains, as before,' (see NIV footnote). This passage is supposed to be a prophecy of an outpouring of the Spirit at Pentecost and again just before the Second Coming. However, the Pentecostal/charismatic would find it difficult to prove that this is in fact what the passage teaches. The passage would seem to be symbolic of the blessings to be poured out after the plagues and disaster of the previous chapter.

There is a similar passage in James which again speaks of autumn and spring rains (5:7,8) but this is a picture of the patience required while the church waits for the Lord's return.

Unfortunately Pentecostal/charismatic teachers are inclined to tear verses out of context to prove their own theories and, to the uninitiated and simple and to those who have not got a firm grasp of the Scriptures, these proofs often seem very convincing. However, when one examines the context of a passage or consults another version of the Bible and compares it with the preacher's translation, the argument will often collapse.

The charismatic puts forward several explanations of why for a long period charismata ceased in the church. Some would say that the gifts have continued all through the church age and have never ceased. They cite Montanism, the Jansenists, the Irvingites and others as examples of continuing phenomena. But as we have seen in our historical section, the groups within which these things took place cannot be described as orthodox Christianity. While we must acknowledge that there have been some genuine evangelical Christians who may have manifested a gift, this has by no means been the normal thing down through history.

Others would say that gifts form part of the Great Commission in Mark 16:15–20, but the movement doesn't fulfil all the other signs.

Yet others would say that the gifts are a confirmation of the gospel and, much as miracles were a common occurrence in the early days of the church, so the church needs miracles now to confirm to the world that it is preaching the true gospel. If this were the case there would surely be other signs too, such as liars being struck dead (Acts 5:1–11), unsaved people being blinded (Acts 13:6–12), or prison doors being opened (Acts 12:1–19). These things clearly do not happen and when the world sees Pentecostal miracles it tends to mock (though we cannot deny that some are being converted), for it often sees charismatic behaviour as exaggerated, childish and laughable.

The other popular theory as to why gifts ceased is that the church succumbed to unbelief. For example, Michael Harper quotes John Wesley: 'The cause of their decline [i.e. that of spiritual gifts] was not, as has been vulgarly supposed, because there is no more need for them, because all the world were become Christians . . . the real cause was: the love of many, almost all Christians so called, was waxed cold . . . this was the real cause why the extraordinary gifts of the Holy Spirit were no longer to be found in the Christian church: because the Christians were turned heathen again and had only a dead form left.'[3]

However, as we have seen already, when Wesley came across charismatics in his own societies (and outside), he vigorously opposed them, for he saw clearly that their behaviour did not match the Scriptures.

The great weakness in this argument is that gifts were not given as a result of a special type of faith. There was no list of qualifications before one could receive a gift, apart from the fact that one was a Christian. The gifts in the New Testament were given to each man as the Spirit himself determined (1 Corinthians 12:11).

Did conversions stop because of lack of faith? Certainly not! If they had, the church would have eventually ceased to exist. We cannot pinpoint a time in the history of the church when some group (however small and persecuted) was not preaching the true gospel and when souls were not being saved. If there was sufficient faith for salvation, there was also sufficient faith to receive the gifts of the Spirit (if this was the correct and scriptural thing to do). The reception of the gifts in the New Testament nowhere required a special measure of faith; the gifts were distributed entirely at the will of our sovereign God and upon whom he chose. There was no outbreak of charismatic phenomena among the Reformers — in spite of the faith which caused them to stand against the corrupt cruelty and savagery of the church of Rome.

13.
Guidance

We will now deal with a number of instances of guidance within the charismatic movement. The charismatic believes in very definite guidance by 'a word from the Lord'. This may come from the Bible, from another person (believer or unbeliever), or from the individual's own mind. Some of these ways of guidance are quite laughable; others border uncomfortably on the occult.

We have already met Demos Shakarian in our historical survey and have seen that he came from an Armenian Pentecostal background. We have seen already how a major prophecy was given to an illiterate eleven-year-old boy which resulted in many Armenian Christians emigrating to the United States. This prophecy came to the boy in the form of a vision. He saw diagrams and pictures and he wrote down the words that he saw, even though he could not read or write. The document is still in existence (together with another secret or sealed prophecy which has still not been opened). This prophecy did come true and those who followed the guidance given in it were saved from the holocaust which came when the Turks tried to annihilate the Armenians.[1]

Mr Shakarian also tells of the way the Armenian Pentecostals sought guidance in their meetings. They met with an open Bible in the middle of the meeting. In prayer the Lord would be asked for specific guidance over some problem by giving the believers 'a word'. The whole congregation would often pray in tongues all at the same time (this is now common practice in the charismatic movement, in spite of the

limits imposed by 1 Corinthians 14:26—28).[2] One of the
elders of the group would then step up to the Bible and
place his finger on a passage at random. The group would
take this as their guidance.[3]

A woman interviewed by Dr Kildahl tells that if she could
not find her scissors, 'She would pray in tongues, close her
eyes while standing in the middle of a room, and turn around
rapidly several times until she felt like stopping. Whatever
way that she faced when she stopped was the direction in
which the Lord wanted her to walk in order to find her
scissors.' If she didn't find the scissors, she assumed the
Lord wanted her to do something else.[4]

Much of what passes for guidance in the neo-Pentecostal
movement is very similar to the phenomenon in occult groups.
At a late stage in my charismatic experience I used to use
the Oxford Group's[5] technique of sitting with a pencil and
notebook waiting for specific guidance from God. Some
mornings this would be a few sentences, but at other times
the words flowed out and covered several pages of a notebook. These words were not paraded to others as a word to
them, but kept for private guidance. This technique was
advocated at a public meeting by a Dr McCall, a charismatic
psychiatrist[6] (see Appendix).

There are a number of men who advocate guidance by
visions and claim that the Lord has appeared to them
regularly throughout their ministry. One such man is Kenneth
E. Hagin, a well-known charismatic speaker from the U.S.A.
His books are publicized in the Christian Literature Crusade
shop near St Paul's Cathedral in London, where they take
up about two shelves. In his autobiography *I believe in
Visions*[7] Mr Hagin tells of a number of visions he has had
of the Lord Jesus Christ. These visions have occurred at
specific times when the Lord has wanted to change the
emphasis of the ministry. It seems significant that one vision
countermands a previous vision and this seems to happen
frequently in charismatic visions.

While we should not discount altogether the possibility

of the Lord appearing to someone in a vision, or guiding someone in some way through a vision, many charismatics believe that this is a normal way of guidance. There is also the tendency, with those who have a powerful imagination, to suppose that the mental pictures they think up are visions. I was at one time the source of a number of these pictures and, while the context of some of them was quite scriptural, they were nevertheless only pictures in the head and not visions. Unfortunately, men like Mr Hagin encourage people to look for this kind of experience and some believe that they are missing out if they are not subject to visions.

We must be content to be guided in what might seem a less spectacular way. God *will* guide us, through his Spirit who dwells within us and through his Word. We will not have to look constantly for the spectacular guidance of a vision, golden letters in the sky, the words of Scripture lighting up, voices (internal or external), as well as specific personal prophecies or words of wisdom or knowledge. God *will* guide us, but visions are very rare, even in the Scriptures.

14.
Initiation into the experience of the baptism of the Holy Spirit

The central doctrine of the charismatic movement is the 'second experience' of 'the baptism of the Holy Spirit'. This 'baptism' supposedly takes place after conversion, in some cases many years later.

Some evangelicals teach a second experience, too, notably the late Dr Martin Lloyd-Jones. In *Joy Unspeakable* he says, 'The great purpose of the baptism with the Spirit is to enable us to witness and to bear testimony to the great salvation that God has granted us through Jesus Christ.' He goes on to state that this baptism 'is essentially a baptism with power'. The evidence of this baptism is, he says, the ability and boldness to witness to the truth.

The charismatic teacher will emphasize that there will be some kind of 'initial evidence'. To the early Pentecostals this initial evidence was speaking in tongues. In the charismatic movement it may be thought to be tongues, prophecy, or feelings of numbness or euphoria.

The problem that arises when this 'second experience' theory is taught is that it encourages people to look for a particular kind of evidence that the experience has actually taken place. To encourage a 'convert', who has produced no fruit of the Spirit in his life, into thinking that a few incoherent sounds, a tingling sensation, fainting, and so on, are proofs that the Spirit has come upon him is very dangerous. What we must see in the new believer is the evidence of a changed life.

Scripture shows that baptism — water or Spirit — is

something that occurs at the beginning of the Christian's life. Baptism with water is associated with beginning to follow either John the Baptist or, more importantly, the Lord Jesus.

Paul says in Colossians 2:12 that we were 'buried with [Christ] in baptism and raised with him through [our] faith in the power of God, who raised him from the dead'.

The context here is that we were dead in sin and have now, in Christ, been raised to a new life by God (see also Romans 6). This is symbolized in baptism. This is clearly the beginning, not a second experience.

John the Baptist mentions baptism in water in the same breath as baptism in the Spirit: 'I baptize you with water for repentance. But after me will come one who is more powerful than I . . . He will baptize you with the Holy Spirit and with fire' (Matthew 3:11). The clear implication is that baptism in water, administered at the beginning of one's discipleship, is typical of the baptism with the Spirit, which also takes place at conversion.[1]

The belief in this 'second experience' has led to many different methods being worked out as to how to reach the experience. The early Pentecostals held what they described as 'tarrying meetings'. People would gather after a formal meeting and pray and agonize for hours on end until they received the experience for which they had craved. The evidence of the reception of the Spirit was the ability to speak in tongues, the so-called 'initial evidence'.

The charismatic movement does not have 'tarrying meetings' as such, but there are many encouragements for the newly converted Christian to seek this experience. With some the experience is initiated in a meeting, the atmosphere tense and expectant, often with the added aid of the laying on of hands. Even with those who do not 'receive' in this way, there is nearly always some psychological pressure to seek and expect the experience. In very many cases there are physical manifestations of some sort — numbness, an electrifying charge in the air, feelings of euphoria or ecstasy, loss of control over the limbs, trembling, burning sensations, chills, excessive perspiration, falling down and occasionally a trance-like condition.

After an evening church service Bill stayed behind with a few others to 'discuss the gift of tongues'. Later this group was asked if any of them would like to receive the gift of speaking in tongues. Bill was one of those keen to do so. They knelt at the altar rail and prayed. The visiting speaker prayed in tongues and went round the group, praying and laying hands on each one. The leader repeated some words which Bill repeated after him and eventually he was speaking in tongues on his own. He was so elated that he wept. They do not appear to have been tears of repentance, but of joy that he had had the experience.[2]

Another man testified, 'I was at home alone when I received the gift of tongues. I had been prayed for at several meetings in church, but didn't receive the gift then. About two weeks after one of these meetings, I received word that my only son was in trouble. As soon as I hung up the 'phone after talking with him, I opened my Bible and began to read out loud from First Corinthians. Suddenly some unknown speech took over, and I couldn't break in on it to read again in English. A power had taken hold of my tongue and words just flowed like water. What a joy it was! There was a feeling of supercleanliness. I have never been the same since.'[3]

Someone else testified, 'The only time that I felt anything in a particular physical way was the first time that I spoke in tongues. At that time I felt a burning all through me, and chills and beads of perspiration, trembling and sort of a weakness in my limbs. Still, I felt wonderful and clean.'[4]

The testimony that follows is from a former missionary in China, Raymond Frame. He attended a meeting at a Chinese Pentecostal church: 'When one of my missionary associates standing beside me suddenly became agitated and began shouting loudly in excellent Chinese, leaping and waving his arms and obviously under the control of a power quite beyond himself, my resistance weakened. I didn't want to be left out of the blessing he was receiving. I let my mind become quite blank and began yielding myself to the external power outside myself that seemed to be pleading for full control of me.

'At once a feeling of paralysis began to numb my feet. It soon affected my legs. I knew that before long I would be lying helpless on the floor as were several others in the crowd. At the instant the numbness reached my knees, I became alarmed. "This thing is coming upon me not from heaven, but from beneath. This is the wrong direction," I thought to myself. Without a moment's hesitation, I cried out, "May the blood of Christ protect me from this thing!" At once it vanished and I was normal again.'[5]

Demos Shakarian, of whom we have spoken earlier, had his 'baptism' while still a young boy. He felt as if someone had placed a heavy woollen blanket over his shoulders. It was so real that he looked round, but no one had touched him. When he tried to move his arms, he felt as if he was pulling them through water. He spoke in tongues.[6]

Alec Taylor, another ex-charismatic, now pastor of a church in Birmingham, tells how he had been in countless 'tarrying meetings' seeking the 'baptism'. 'The choruses,' he writes, 'such as "Spirit of the Living God, fall afresh on me," the hand clapping, shouts of "Jesus, Jesus, Jesus!" and the Hallelujahs help many to a state of ecstasy where it is easy to let one's tongue loose.' Mr Taylor did not experience his 'baptism' this way, however, and it was at a smaller, less public meeting that he had hands laid upon him and he spoke in tongues.[7]

These experiences, while clearly very real to those who have them, are not really comparable with Scripture. All those in the Bible upon whom the Spirit came certainly experienced something. This we do not deny.

Isaiah saw the Lord sitting upon his throne, but he reported no paralysis, or burning sensations. He could only cry out, 'Woe to me! . . . For I am a man of unclean lips, and I live among a people of unclean lips' (Isaiah 6:5).

When the Spirit came upon Ezekiel, he again did not report any peculiar physical phenomena, though he most certainly experienced something (Ezekiel 3).

John the Baptist was filled with the Holy Spirit from his mother's womb and, while he undoubtedly was led by the Spirit to live a strange kind of existence, yet no burning sensations or tremblings or other peculiar phenomena were reported of him.

When Jesus was baptized in Jordan, the Holy Spirit descended like a dove and rested upon him, but again there was no odd behaviour (Matthew 3:13–17; Mark 1:9–13; Luke 3:21–22; John 1:29–34).

On the Day of Pentecost the disciples spoke in tongues, but there is no report of burning sensations (in spite of the tongues of fire), no 'Pentecostal' behaviour; everything appears to have been done 'in a fitting and orderly way'. Even the accusation of drunkenness (Acts 2:13) was only aimed at them because certain bystanders could not understand all that was being said. There is no record of strange antics from any of the large number converted after Peter's Pentecost sermon – indeed, everything is remarkably orderly.

Philip's campaign to Samaria was accompanied by signs and wonders, and we are told that evil spirits came out of many 'with shrieks', so we may be sure that the meetings would have been noisy, but there doesn't appear to have been any peculiar behaviour when later the Holy Spirit came upon them (Acts 8:14–17).

When the Ethiopian eunuch was was converted through the ministry of Philip, on the road to Gaza, he asked to be baptized. It is inconceivable that Philip would have sent him back to a heathen country completely unaided by the Holy Spirit (for there is no record that Philip mentioned the Holy Spirit). We must assume that the conversion of this gentleman also meant that he was filled with the Holy Spirit and with his Scriptures he was fully equipped to labour for the gospel in the Ethopian field.

Let us challenge any Pentecostal or charismatic who reads this book to prove from Scripture that the physical phenomena known so widely in the charismatic movement are compatible with the experience of the saints in the Bible.

15.
The charismatic movement, Roman Catholicism and unity

The view of a large number of charismatic preachers and teachers is that the Roman Catholic Church is a part of God's true church on earth. It is clear that the major part of the charismatic movement does not hold the view of the Reformers. Michael Harper, a prominent Church of England charismatic, believes that the things which divide Roman Catholics, evangelicals and charismatics are less weighty than the things which unite them.[1] He also believes, and here he is probably representative of a large number of other charismatics, that God's plan for the salvation of mankind cannot be fulfilled without the Roman church.[2]

It is difficult to see how a church which still claims to be the one true church, which calls its head 'the Vicar of Christ on earth', which insists that the mass is 'the unbloody renewal of the sacrifice of the cross' and whose devotees pray to Mary, Queen of Heaven, can claim to be a true church at all. All these things, and much else besides, are entirely without scriptural foundation.

The problem would seem to lie in the attitude of the charismatic and the Roman Catholic to the Bible. The Roman Catholic believes that the Bible is the Word of God, but that it is to be interpreted in accordance with the tradition of the church (that is, of course, the Roman church); the charismatic also believes that the Bible is the Word of God, though it must be interpreted charismatically. Some would teach that it only becomes the Word of God to you when God gives you a special revelation of a particular part of it. This is close to so-called neo-orthodoxy.

Can we say that the Roman doctrine of the mass, for example, is a justifiable interpretation of Scripture, or is it a blasphemous and idolatrous feast? Some charismatics would take the Reformed position with regard to the mass, the virgin Mary and much else besides, but many are quite happy to go along with Roman Catholic doctrine. But there is only one truth. Two opposite opinions cannot both be right, though some charismatics come close to saying they can be.

A large section of the charismatic movement sees the question of unity as a vital issue, which must be settled as soon as possible and at any price. Many seem to be prepared to find the lowest common denominator and to unite on that. And it must be unity with Rome. There is much talk of unity and there is sometimes a kind of unity manifested. Michael Harper tells of a meeting held in Sydney, Australia, attended by Roman Catholics, charismatics and classical Pentecostals. The meeting was advertised as a 'healing service'. The main speakers were Francis McNutt (an American Roman Catholic priest) and Tommy Tyson (an American Methodist). Both men spoke of the power of forgiveness and then led the meeting in an act of confession. Francis McNutt confessed the sins Catholics had committed against Protestants and Tommy Tyson confessed the sins that Protestants had committed against Roman Catholics. Michael Harper continues, 'There was much weeping that night. We felt the pain of separation. We felt the hurts in the Body of Christ, the wounds that mar the beauty of the Bride of Christ, but wounds that were being healed before our eyes.'[3] But what was the end result of this meeting and this repentance after the tears had dried up and the conferees had departed their several ways? Did any Roman Catholic begin to examine his Bible and consequently give up going to mass and stop worshipping the virgin Mary? We cannot say, but there seems to have been no pressure for him to do so.

There are charismatics who have gone so far as to say that they believe that the Reformation was a dreadful mistake.

David Watson, a charismatic Church of England minister
said it was 'one of the greatest tragedies since Pentecost'.[4]
It is difficult to find words to express the horror and despair
which grips one as these words are read. Did he really mean
it? What of all the simple believers who lost their lives standing for the truth as it is revealed in Scripture? What of those
who were tried, condemned as heretics, tortured upon the
rack or burned at the stake? Were they mistaken? Was Martin
Luther mistaken about justification by faith? (If he was
mistaken, so was Paul!) Were the Anabaptists wrong to insist
on believers' baptism? Were they all wrong in insisting that
the Bible is the Word of God? The Reformation was a time
when the Bible, which had been a sealed book in the hands
of a largely corrupt clergy, was once again put into the hands
of common believers. Was this a tragedy? No! A thousand
times, 'No'! We must insist that they were right in obeying
the scriptural injunction to 'come out from them and be
separate, says the Lord. Touch no unclean thing, and I will
receive you' (2 Corinthians 6:17).

If Luther, Calvin and others had stayed in the Roman
church, which is what the charismatics seem to suggest, what
would have happened? They would have been exiled in some
monastery or put into prison or burned; their books would
have been destroyed and their words heard no more. They
and their works would have vanished from the face of the
earth. But evangelicals believe that these men (though they
made mistakes) were guided by the Holy Spirit to separate
themselves from Rome and far from being a tragedy, it was a
glorious triumph of the Son of God!

The present pope, John Paul II, has caught the public eye
in a big way since he was enthroned. Some charismatics seem
to see him as a great boost to Christianity and refer to him
as a 'man of God' and 'God's man for the hour'. A charismatic told me in conversation that John Paul II was a true
Christian because he could say, 'Christ is Lord' (see Romans
10:9). However, he would seem rather to be a devotee of the
virgin Mary. In every country that he has travelled to since

becoming pope, the places that he has visited have included the centres of Mariolatry. In Mexico he visited the Shrine of Our Lady of Guadaloupe, in Poland he paid homage to the Black Madonna of Czestochowa and in Eire he visited the village and shrine of Knock. On the day Karol Wojtyla was declared pope he said, 'I was afraid to accept this choice, but I did so in a spirit of humility and obedience to our Lord and complete trust in His most Holy Mother, the Madonna.' And he vowed, 'I . . . make profession of our common faith, our hope and trust in the mother of Christ, and the mother of the Church . . .'[5]

The 'charismatic renewal' has now become widely established in the Roman Catholic Church. It is reputedly the best organized of the denominational charismatic groups.[6] Michael Harper has said that the birth of the Catholic charismatic movement was 'small and largely unheralded. But within a very short time it was to be the dominant force in the charismatic world, wielding an influence throughout the whole world . . .'[7] If this claim is true, then it is no wonder that there is a constant effort to unite under one flag. Rome is very keen that all should be united under one banner and that the pope should be acknowledged as the head of the one church.

Testimonies of many Catholic charismatics show that they have not been released from the beliefs and practices common to all Roman Catholics. Here are some examples: 'Attendance at Mass has grown to be my way of life. Through the Mass I receive the strength to witness to Christ, and His teachings.'[8] 'I have returned to frequent confession, where before I was doubtful of its value as a corrective agent.'[9] 'Traditional devotions such as those to Mary have become more meaningful to me (and I am one who put Mary completely out of the picture many years ago).'[10] A student reports that since his 'baptism in the Spirit' he prays the rosary between classes.[11]

Sadly, the charismatic experience is drawing some people brought up as Protestants into Roman Catholic practices.

While I would not deny Roman Catholics and/or charismatics the liberty of worship as they see fit, I must state that the spirit which guides the Roman Catholic and the charismatic is a different spirit from the one who guides the evangelical Christian. I would maintain that the Spirit who guided holy men of God to write down the Scriptures is the same Spirit who inspires the evangelical believer. The Spirit who inspired the Scriptures will not deny himself by guiding people to do things which he has forbidden. The Holy Spirit cannot deny or contradict himself.

16.
Is the charismatic movement a revival?

As we saw briefly in an earlier chapter, the charismatic move-movement is sometimes referred to as 'the charismatic revival' and sometimes writers sympathetic to the movement have sought to explain it in terms of revival. If we compare the movement with revivals of the past, revivals which charismatics themselves would recognize as movements of the Spirit, we shall be able to see clearly whether it is revival or not.

First of all, we need to have a definition of what revival is. Duncan Campbell, a man experienced in revival, defined it as 'a community saturated with God'.[1] Emyr Roberts defines revival as 'the conviction and conversion of a great number of people, taking place contemporaneously, publicly and very often dramatically, to the great increase and expansion of the Church. There is no fundamental, qualitative difference between the work of the Spirit in the case of one individual and the work of the Spirit in that which we call revival, but only a difference of degree. Both are the work of the same Spirit of God; both are equally miraculous and supernatural, like the mystery of the wind "which bloweth where it listeth"!'[2]

There are a number of features noticeable in times of revival. Firstly, *there are areas where the presence of God can be felt.* Pastor Harry Waite says that 'There are areas of the presence of God, into which you can move geographically and out of which you can come . . .' And he continues, 'Not everyone is saved in a revival but everyone is conscious of the presence of God.'[3] This geographical presence can be illustrated many times from the records of past revivals. Pastor Waite, in the same sermon, tells the story of a Lancashire man and his two daughters who travelled to Wales in 1904 to witness the revival for themselves. They were heading for Rhos just outside Wrexham. 'They came off the train at Chester and got into the train for Wrexham and they said to the platform attendant, because they were strangers, "How will we know when we get to Wrexham?" and without hesitation the station man said, "You'll feel it," and they didn't quite understand what he meant, but as they drew near to Wrexham they felt the presence of God in the train.'[4]

During the Hebrides revival in 1949 we are told that 'The presence of God was a universal, inescapable fact, at home, in the church and by the roadside. Many who visited Lewes during this period became vividly conscious of the spiritual atmosphere before they reached the island.'[5] One man came to a minister in great concern for his soul. The minister asked him, '"What touched you? I haven't seen you at any of the services." "No!" he replied, "I haven't been to church but this revival is in the air, I can't get away from the Spirit."'[6]

A second feature is that *people became very concerned about eternal issues and over the state of their souls.* Jonathan Edwards, in his famous *Narrative*, states that 'There scarcely was a single person in the town, old or young, left unconcerned about the great things of the eternal world . . . This work of God . . . soon made a great alteration in the town; so that in the spring and summer following and 1735, the town seemed to be full of the presence of God: it never was so full of love, nor of joy, and yet so full of distress, as it was then.'[7]

In another place Edwards relates, 'Persons are sometimes brought to the borders of despair, and it looks as black as midnight to them a little before the day dawns in their souls. Some few instances there have been, of persons who have had such a sense of God's wrath for sin, that they have been overborne; and made to cry out under the astonishing sense of their guilt, wondering that God suffers such guilty wretches to live upon earth and that he doth not immediately send them to hell.'[8]

On the island of Lewes there were occasions when the preacher's voice was drowned by the sound of men and women weeping uncontrollably. Sometimes the preaching had to be halted because of the distress of those listening.[9]

In the Hebrides and the New England revivals secular work seems largely to have been set aside for a period because of the great concern over eternal issues.

The same concern and spirit of distress expressed itself in the Korean revival in 1907. The 'Spirit flamed forth and spread till practically every church, not only in North Korea, but throughout the entire peninsula had received its share of the blessing'. The sense of sin was almost overwhelming and even children wept over their wrongdoings. Some went 'from house to house, confessing to individuals they had injured, returning stolen property and money, not only to Christians but to heathen as well, till the whole city (Pyengyang) was stirred'.[10] William Blair, commenting on the confession of serious sins which took place at the time, says, 'Such sins cannot be confessed without the whole nature being torn as with a death struggle . . . [But] the result was everywhere wholesome, except where men deliberately resisted or sought to deceive the Spirit and their brethren.'[11]

Bruce Hunt is keen to point out in the introduction to *The Korean Pentecost* that little charismatic phenomena accompanied this revival. He states, 'It is noteworthy that in Korea itself, and especially in a denomination [Presbyterian] the majority of whose missionaries have recognized the 1907 revival as having had a great influence on church growth, there has been so little of what in the West is known as Pentecostalism. It is only in recent years [this was written in 1977] that the "tongues movement" and the emphasis on "faith healing" have become popular in Korea.'[12]

Thirdly, we note *the joy of the worshippers in a time of*

revival. Past revivals have often been noted for the hymns which have been produced. The hymns of the Wesleys, for example, came largely as a result of the so-called Methodist revival. The revival in Wales in 1904 was another revival where singing played a very large part; in fact, some have criticized this aspect of the revival as it tended to displace the preaching of the Word.[13]

Fourthly, the most important aspect of any revival is *the revelation of the character of God.* Men, women and children have become overwhelmed with the revelation of God by the Holy Spirit in their own souls.

Rev. J. T. Job, a minister in Bethesda, Wales, tells of a night in 1904 when 'I felt the Holy Spirit like a torrent of light causing my whole nature to shake; I saw Jesus Christ — and my nature melted at His feet; and I saw myself — and I abhorred it!'[14]

Jonathan Edwards tells how 'Our young people, when they met, were wont to spend the time in talking of the excellency and dying love of Jesus Christ, the glory of the way of salvation, the wonderful, free and sovereign grace of God, His glorious work in the conversion of a soul, the truth and certainty of the great things of God's Word, the sweetness of the views of His perfections, etc.'[15]

In another place he says, 'Many have spoken much of their hearts being drawn out in love to God and Christ; and of their minds being wrapped up in delightful contemplation of the glory and wonderful grace of God, the excellency and dying love of Jesus Christ; and of their souls going forth in longing desire after God and Christ. Several of our young children have expressed much of this; and have manifested a willingness to leave father and mother and all things in the world to go and be with Christ. Some persons have had such longing desires after Christ as to take away their natural strength. Some have been so overcome with a sense of the dying love of Christ to such poor, wretched, and unworthy creatures, as to weaken the body. Several persons have had a great sense of the glory of God, and excellency of Christ, that nature and life seem almost to sink under it; and in all probability if God had showed them a little more of Himself, it would have dissolved their frame. I have seen some, and conversed with them in such frames, who have certainly been perfectly sober, and very remote from anything like enthusiastic wildness. And they have talked, when able to speak, of the glory of God's perfections, the wonderfulness of His grace in Christ, and their own unworthiness, in such a manner as cannot be perfectly expressed after them. Their sense of their exceeding littleness and vileness, and their disposition to abase themselves before God, has appeared to be great in proportion to their light and joy.'[16]

How do these features compare with the charismatic movement of today?

First of all, I cannot see that it qualifies as a revival if we accept the definitions of Duncan Campbell and Emyr Roberts. The whole community has certainly not been affected.

Secondly, there are no areas where the presence of God may be felt. No doubt the charismatic would claim that the Holy Spirit's presence is felt in their meetings, but unfortunately this does not compare with revival. Very often the feelings to which the charismatic is subject are the result of deliberate pressure brought to bear by the leaders. In other words, it is a manifestation of the flesh, rather than the Spirit.

Thirdly, there is usually no great concern displayed or expressed by converts of the movement or those who claim to have received 'the baptism of the Spirit'. There is no great sense of sin and, while repentance is sometimes taught, it is not stressed very much. Indeed, if a person displays great concern and distress over the state of his soul, he might well be thought to be 'in bondage' or to need some specialized ministry, such as casting out of demons.

Fourthly, while there is considerable 'joy' displayed in meetings, this is often a manifestation of the flesh. There is a light-hearted approach to the worship. Hymns are not used very much; the preference is for very simple (indeed

often childish) choruses. David Pawson suggests that one of
the first signs that God is moving in revival is through music;
indeed he goes so far as to say that this is a proof that God is
moving.[17]

Dancing is also something which occurs frequently in
charismatic meetings, especially the larger gatherings. It is
encouraged by leaders like David Pawson and again is looked
upon as a sign that the Spirit is moving. Sadly much of this
dancing is clearly a manifestation of natural exuberance,
that is, it is of the flesh. It is also interesting to note that
'dancing in the Spirit' can be learned rather as tongues can
be learned. While there are references to dancing in the Old
Testament, there are none in the New Testament which
suggest that the early disciples danced in their meetings. It
is noticeable too that very few manifestations of dancing
have occurred during historic revivals. One exception would
be the Welsh revival of 1762. This manifestation appears to
have been 'the practice of jumping in response to the Word
preached',[18] a practice which gave rise to the nickname
'Welsh Jumpers'. This phenomenon would seem to have
little in common with 'dancing in the Spirit' as practised
by the charismatic movement.

Lastly, and more seriously, the character of the God
revealed by the charismatic movement is often a caricature
of the God revealed in Scripture. He is not a God to be
feared. Charismatics are fond of quoting the verse: 'Perfect
love drives out fear' (1 John 4:18). He loves everyone and
doesn't seem too concerned over sin; indeed if some charismatics are to be believed he seems to encourage it on
occasions.

Some charismatic teachers suggest that God is a God
who puts himself at the disposal of the Christian; we can
give him orders. Dr Yonggi Cho, the Korean Pentecostal
minister, in his strange book *The Fourth Dimension* tells how
he encouraged a spinster who desired to get married to 'order
a husband from God'. They mapped out together what this
husband would be like — Caucasian, tall, skinny, musical, a

schoolteacher, etc. Dr Cho then told her to read this list to the Lord until she received what she wanted.[19] Is the God whom we can manipulate in this way the God of the Bible?

We in the churches of the West need a revival desperately. We need a fresh revelation of the character of the God we worship, a revelation of his holiness, his majesty and his grace. It has not come through the charismatic movement, although this movement claims it is 'a movement of the Spirit of God'.

17.
Testimonies of men who have come out of second blessing movements

There follow here a number of testimonies of men who have been in 'second blessing' or charismatic groups.

James Davenport

James Davenport was born in 1716 in New England. He graduated from Yale in 1732 at the age of sixteen. At twenty-two he was ordained minister of the Presbyterian Church in Southold, Long Island. He met and became friendly with George Whitefield, the English Methodist evangelist, while Whitefield was on a tour of America. He was influenced by Whitefield and Whitefield seems to have been impressed by Davenport. Whitefield said that 'Of all men living, he knew of none who kept a closer walk with God.'

Davenport was impressed by the revival power manifested whenever George Whitefield or his fellow evangelists preached. He sought to promote revival in his own church, but his methods were extravagant. At one stage he gathered his congregation together and preached to them for almost twenty-four hours non-stop. Afterwards he was exhausted and went into seclusion for several days. Some of the congregation, however, made professions of faith and therefore he felt that his methods were justified.

These converts Davenport now began to address as 'brother' or 'sister' and all other church members as plain 'Mister', 'Mrs' or 'neighbour'. He forbade the 'neighbours' to attend the Lord's Table. Thus Davenport developed a two-tier church — the 'spiritual' and the 'carnal'. This is what has often happened in a number of churches influenced by the charismatic movement.

In 1741 Davenport held meetings in North Stonington, Connecticut. He met the pastor of the church, Joseph Fish, but was not impressed with him. Mr Fish had witnessed an awakening in his own congregation, but Davenport believed him to be spiritually dead. Fish resented Davenport, as he had come into the parish uninvited, so there was antagonism between the two men. Under Davenport's ministry some were converted and again the two-tier system developed. Davenport's converts gathered around him, while others in the congregation remained loyal to their pastor. Davenport began to encourage his followers to leave the church. Ninety-two left and helped to organize a new congregation, which eventually grew to four hundred. This move brought an end to the revival.

His treatment of the pastors he came into contact with during his itinerant ministry, like Joseph Fish, was shameful. He believed that those who did not give him their unqualified support had to be broken down, discredited and humiliated.

Davenport put great emphasis at this stage in his career on guidance by visions, trances and direct impressions from texts of Scripture and regarded these as infallible evidence of the Holy Spirit working in the Christian.

While on a visit to Boston he met with an assembly of ministers of the gospel, who examined him regarding his life and work. These godly evangelical ministers believed that he had been wrong to criticize his fellow ministers and to lead his followers in extravagant forms of worship. They agreed together that he would not be invited to preach in any of their churches.

In 1742 he was arrested and committed for trial charged with neglecting his pastoral duties in his own congregation. A number of ministers wrote to the court asking that Davenport be treated gently. The grand jury's verdict was that he was not in his right mind and therefore not guilty.

He continued itinerating and in March 1743 he arrived in New London to organize a new church, at the request of a number of his followers. On his arrival, he claimed that he had received special guidance from God in dreams. He made an effort to 'purify' the congregation, even giving out a list of books which must be burned. This list included the works of such notable writers as Beveridge, Flavel and Increase Mather.

By the summer of 1744, Davenport had come to his senses, due to the labours of a number of godly pastors who had sought to draw him from the errors into which he had fallen. He confessed his folly in a remarkable document, *The Rev. Mr Davenport's Retractions*. This document contains the following moving passage: 'I confess I have been much led astray by following impulses and impressions as a rule of conduct, whether they come with or without a text of Scripture; and my neglecting, also, duly to observe the analogy of Scripture. I am persuaded this was a great means of corrupting my experiences and carrying me off from the Word of God, and a great handle, which the false spirit has made use of with respect to a number, and me especially.'

Davenport had twice been judged insane by the civil authorities and it is apparent that he was in a poor state of health. His poor health had caused him to be subject to flights of fancy and vivid dreams. He aggravated this by going without sleep, spending whole nights in prayer and constant preaching. In his weakened state it is not surprising that his mind was in turmoil. By 1744, with the opportunity for rest, his health improved. During this period, with the assistance of two ministers, he became convinced of his errors and published his *Retractions*. Afterwards he moved to New Jersey and laboured faithfully in the gospel, but lived for only a few years longer.

Sadly, not many charismatics have been persuaded of their errors as Davenport was. Perhaps evangelicals need to be more compassionate towards charismatics and to take the time and trouble to counsel them from the Scriptures.[1]

Henry Ironside

Henry Ironside was born in Toronto, Canada, into a Christian family. His father died while Henry was still a baby and his mother took him to live in Los Angeles, California.

By the time Henry was twelve years old, he had started his own Sunday School, though he was still not a Christian. However, he was a keen Bible student, having read the Bible through some ten times. At the age of fourteen a minister, visiting his home, asked him if he had been born again. He knew that the only honest answer that he could give was 'No'. So convicted was he by this question that, in an endeavour to stifle his conscience, he went into sin. His conscience, however, continued to trouble him.

About six months later, he relates how matters reached crisis point: 'On a Thursday evening in February 1890, God spoke to me in tremendous power while at a party with a lot of other young people ... Standing alone by a refreshment table, there came home to my inmost soul in startling clearness, some verses of Scripture I had learned months before. They are found in the first chapter of Proverbs, beginning with verse 24 and going on to verse 32. Here wisdom is represented as laughing at the calamity of the one who refused to heed instruction, and mocking when his fear cometh. Every word seemed to burn its way into my heart. I saw as never before my dreadful guilt in having so long refused to trust Christ myself, and in having preferred my own wilful way to that of Him who had died for me.'

Later that evening Henry hurried home and went to his room. He took down his Bible and read Romans 3 and John 3. Rereading John 3:16, he prayed, 'O God, I thank Thee that Thou hast loved me, and given Thy Son for me. I trust Him now as my Saviour; and I rest on Thy Word, which tells me

I have everlasting life.' Though he was disappointed that he did not 'feel' anything, he took the Bible at its word and rose from his knees to begin his walk of faith.

He desired, as a young Christian, to lead others to the Saviour and to this end he joined up with the Salvation Army. He rapidly came to be known as 'the boy preacher', which he admits ministered to his pride.

In spite of his preaching he longed for perfect victory over his lusts and desires and after about eight months became interested in special holiness meetings. Here he was introduced to the doctrine of 'the second blessing'. He was taught that, after a person was converted, God forgave all sins committed up to the point when the believer repented. The Christian was then placed on lifelong probation during which period it was possible to fall away and to lose one's justification. The only safeguard against this was for the believer to enter into a further work of grace which would deal with the root of sin.

The steps to this were (1) conviction of the need for holiness, (2) a full surrender, (3) claiming 'in faith the incoming of the Holy Spirit as a refining fire to burn out all inbred sin, thus destroying *in toto* every lust and passion, leaving the soul perfect in love and pure as unfallen Adam'. Coupled [with this teaching] were heartfelt testimonies of experiences so remarkable that I could not doubt their genuineness . . .'

At this time he heard the testimony of an elderly lady, who claimed that she had not sinned in thought, word or deed for forty years. 'Her heart, she claimed, was no longer "deceitful above all things and desperately wicked," but was as holy as the courts of heaven, since the blood of Christ had washed away the last remains of inbred sin.' Henry began to seek this blessing for himself. He prayed, read and organized for the blessing of Adamic sinlessness.

One Saturday night, he went into the country resolved not to return until he had received the blessing of perfect love. Under a tree he agonized in prayer for hours.

Eventually he fell almost fainting to the ground and 'a holy ecstasy seemed to thrill all my being'. He believed that the Holy Spirit had come upon him. He prayed, 'Lord, I believe Thou dost come in. Thou dost cleanse and purify me from all sin. I claim it now. The work is done. I am sanctified by Thy blood. Thou dost make me holy. I believe; I believe.' He was very happy and sure that his struggles were ended. He attended meetings at which he testified to his new-found holiness; he noticed afterwards that his own experience became the theme, rather than the Lord Jesus.

Henry was still very young and at sixteen he became a cadet in the Salvation Army and went for training to an Army garrison. There he began to have problems keeping in his holiness. He was greatly troubled when he believed he had backslidden and upon confession and claiming by faith that he was cleansed again he would be better for a few weeks, but then he gradually slipped again and the whole process was repeated. He went through a period of some eighteen months, struggling against his lower nature, striving to enter and hold onto the blessing and then falling away again. A companion in his sufferings, 'one of the loveliest souls' he had ever met, eventually fell away completely and became a spiritualist.

He goes on: 'I began to see what a string of derelicts this holiness teaching left in its train. I could count scores of persons who had gone into utter infidelity because of it. They always gave the same reason: "I tried it all. I found it a failure. So I concluded the Bible teaching was a delusion and religion was a mere matter of the emotions." Many more (and I knew several such intimately) lapsed into insanity after floundering in the morass of this emotional religion for years – and people said that studying the Bible had driven them crazy. How little they knew that it was lack of Bible knowledge that was accountable for their wretched mental state – an absolutely unscriptural use of isolated passages of Scripture!'

At last he decided that he must resign from the Army,

but was persuaded by his commanding officer to stay on for six months. He was driven to despair due to his constant mental anguish and his run-down physical condition. He was at last sent to an Army rest home. Here he expected an atmosphere of great devotion and holiness, but found that an air of carelessness pervaded the place.

While at the home he met a girl lieutenant, who he believed had the blessing of full sanctification. During a long conversation, however, she confessed that she had struggled for years to obtain the blessing but had not. They came to the conclusion that their failure was because they had struggled to become holy in their own strength. Together they began to search the Scriptures. Soon afterwards Henry and the lieutenant found their doubts and fears removed, as they were taken up with Christ alone.

Mr Ironside's comments on the holiness movement at the turn of the century are a solemn warning to Christians today. This was a time when those who held holiness doctrines were beginning to practise 'the gifts of the Spirit'.

He makes some very unflattering remarks about the circles in which he had formerly moved. He says that those who profess to be holy are frequently uncharitable and harsh, prone to exaggeration or downright dishonesty and their preachers are often given to levity and amusing sermons. His remarks on the tongues aspect of the movement are even more cutting. He claims that the movement (in the early 1900s) was attended by delusions and insanities: 'An unhealthy craving for new and thrilling religious sensations, and emotional meetings of a most exciting character, readily account for these things.' He concludes, 'Let a full Christ be preached, a finished work be proclaimed, the truth of the indwelling Spirit be Scripturally taught, and all these excrescences disappear.'[2]

Wong Ming-Dao

Wong Ming-Dao was born in Peking, China, during the Boxer

Rebellion in 1900. His father committed suicide during the seige of the Legation Quarter by the Boxers and troops of the ruling Ching Dynasty. His mother, sisters and Wong himself survived the seige.[3] He was later educated at a modernist Presbyterian mission school, but while there was converted, at the age of fourteen, through the testimony of another pupil. At this time he came under great conviction of sin.

By 1921 Wong Ming-Dao had seen from the Scriptures that believers should be baptized by immersion. Upon informing the school authorities (he was now a teacher) that he wished to be baptized by immersion, he was asked to leave. A few days later he was baptized in a local river with a group of others.

The man who baptized him was a Mr Ju, a Pentecostal preacher. As soon as the little group had been baptized, Mr Ju exhorted them to seek the Holy Spirit. Soon afterwards Wong Ming-Dao's companions spoke in tongues, but it was not until several days afterwards that his tongue 'produced some incomprehensible sounds and Mr Ju announced 'that I was speaking in tongues and that I had received the Holy Spirit'.[4] He goes on to tell how Mr Ju had taught the group to shout 'Hallelujah!' and to repeat it over and over without stopping. He came to the conclusion that it was tongues manufactured by man.[5]

Soon after these incidents he had the opportunity for prolonged Bible reading and study and the Lord, by his grace, opened Wong's understanding of the Word.[6]

He did for some time preach the Pentecostal doctrine of 'the baptism of the Holy Spirit', the evidence of which was speaking in tongues. However, doubts arose in his mind when he came across people who simply repeated 'one sound such as "Ba – ba – ba – ba" or "Da – da – da – da" or "Go-di, go-di, go-di, go-di", for several tens of minutes, always repeating the same sounds. I ask, how can you call this "tongues"? Even when angels speak they cannot use just one or two sounds to express many meanings . . . Another problem is that the manner of life of many who speak in tongues is particularly bad.'[7]

He also saw that, as those who claimed to be filled with the Spirit did not live in the Spirit, some who did not claim to be filled with the Spirit lived lives of power and authority. 'Can it be that they did not possess the Holy Spirit?' he asked. These doubts caused him to give up his Pentecostal teachings.[8]

Wong Ming-Dao became a leader of the church in China and was later imprisoned for his faith by the Communist authorities. After twenty-three years without a Bible or any Christian fellowship, he was released from prison in 1980.

George Gardiner

In the introduction to his very helpful book *Corinthian Catastrophe*, Mr Gardiner gives a brief testimony. He graduated from a Pentecostal Bible School. Later in his life he became disillusioned with the Pentecostal movement and began to question why there was such a gulf between charismatic practices and scriptural statements? He found that to question things in this way was liable to bring warnings of 'sin against the Holy Spirit'.

During four years of war service, when he was isolated from other Christians, Mr Gardiner faced up to his doubts. He had no book but the Bible. He read through the Acts of the Apostles slowly and carefully, praying, as he did so, that the Lord would guide him. He describes the journey through Acts as 'an eye-opener! The actions and experiences of the early churches were far removed from the actions and "experiences" of the modern movement. In some ways they were completely opposite! There were no "tarrying meetings" preceding and precipitating Pentecost. The disciples were commanded to "wait" — the most non-strenuous word the Lord could have used. When the Holy Spirit came they were "sitting", they were not on their knees praying, singing, agonizing, etc. In fact, Pentecost had to come fifty days after Christ's resurrection, regardless of what the people in the upper room were doing! It was ordained by God, as typified in the Old Testament feasts, as recorded in Leviticus 23. First, the Passover: 'Christ our Passover' — then the Feast of the First Fruits: 'Christ the First Fruits' — followed fifty days later by the Feast of Pentecost! For the first time I understood what was meant by the phrase, "When the day of Pentecost was fully come". It did not refer to "tarrying", surrendering, fasting or any other human effort to bring it about — it was God's appointed time!

'I could not find one command anywhere in the New Testament for Christians to seek the baptism of the Holy Spirit. Instead I discovered [as outlined in the section on 1 Corinthians 12] that the "baptism" had occurred when I was placed in the body of Christ at my conversion.'

He came out of the movement 'into the relief and freedom I enjoy today'.[9]

Alec Taylor

Alec Taylor spent fourteen years in the Pentecostal movement. He is now pastor of a Reformed Baptist church in Birmingham.

Mr Taylor testifies to being saved as a teenager and joined a Pentecostal church. After two years of 'seeking' and 'tarrying', he spoke in tongues as hands were laid on him. After a time he began to question the genuineness of his own experience and the experience of others. He had a wide range of experience in Pentecostal circles in the United Kingdom and on the Continent and observed that French tongues had a bias towards French intonations and Dutch tongues towards Dutch intonations. He remarks, 'As a teenager, I was told that someone in our church spoke in Afrikaans when she spoke in tongues. You can imagine how eagerly I looked forward to hearing this Afrikaans again after six months in

Holland with the Royal Air Force, each Sunday in a Pentecostal church. I had grasped enough Dutch to get the gist of
any message in Afrikaans which is, of course, similar. As
I heard the old familiar tongue again, it wasn't remotely
like Afrikaans!' He also found that the same tongues
message would be translated entirely differently from week
to week. However, he persevered in the Pentecostal church
because he feared (like many others), that in questioning
tongues and prophecy he would be blaspheming the Holy
Spirit.

He suffered four years of mental and spiritual turmoil
but came to realize that we should be equally careful about
attributing pathetic claims of charismata to the Spirit when
they are fleshly.[10]

The author's own testimony

I was born in south-east London in 1937 to nominally
Anglican parents. My father became a Freemason later in his
life and my mother has had an interest in spiritualism and
astrology. I was sent to a Church of England school; I cannot
ever remember hearing the gospel plainly preached, though
we attended chapel once a day and twice on Sundays. I was
'christened' at the age of eleven or so, in time to be confirmed – this being the usual practice at school.

As a youngster in my teens I was interested in 'strange'
religions – yoga and witchcraft, among other things, catching
my attention. On entering the R.A.F. for National Service,
I started to read more widely about Eastern religions.
Buddhism became an abiding interest and caught my
imagination as offering some form of sensible philosophy.
It did not seem to be hampered by a necessity to believe
in God. I started to call myself a Buddhist while still in the
R.A.F.

On leaving the service, I eventually settled into the textile
trade, which was my father's occupation. In 1960 a friend

with whom I worked became a Christian and started to talk to me about Jesus. I at first countered this with talk of Buddha, but because of the obvious change in his life (and no doubt through his prayers) I began to read a New Testament. By the grace of God, I began to see that Jesus was indeed the Christ, the Son of the living God. He clearly called me to follow him.

I began to attend a small Congregational church and then a Baptist mission. After a move, my wife and I started to attend a small Open Brethren assembly, where we went forward for believers' baptism. During this period I began to feel the inadequacy of my personal walk with the Lord and longed for a more consistent and effective Christian life. By the grace of God I had, early in my Christian life, come to see that, if Jesus had believed the Old Testament, then I too had no alternative but to accept the Bible as the Word of God. Had I been better taught and more discerning, I would have been saved much heartache later on.

During the early 1960s I came into contact with Pentecostal/charismatic teaching. I had continued to seek something deeper in my spiritual life and came to the view that 'the baptism in the Spirit' was what I needed. I read numerous books on the subject; most seemed to be contradictory.

I attended a meeting in the West End of London where a well-known Pentecostal evangelist was preaching. He laid hands on a number of people for healing. I was not convinced that anything had happened to these people, although the evangelist claimed that they were healed. At the end of the meeting an appeal was given for those who wished to receive 'the baptism'. I and another man went forward. The evangelist laid hands on the other man and prayed that he would receive the Spirit. As he finished praying he said, 'You can now speak in tongues!' The man remained silent. The evangelist was a little impatient and said, 'Come on now! You can do it! Say after me — Abbadabbadabbadabbadabba!' The man repeated the phrase and was told that he was speaking in tongues. I walked out!

However, so great was my hunger and my ignorance that I continued to search for this ultimate experience that would make me a spiritual Christian. I was encouraged to believe, by the books that I read and by the charismatics that I talked to, that this baptism would solve many of my problems and would make my walk with Jesus more real.

In 1964 I attended a meeting at an Assemblies of God church in the East End of London. The service was extremely noisy. Nevertheless I went forward afterwards for the 'baptism'. I was taken into the vestry where the pastor and an elder prayed over me, laying hands on my head. Nothing happened. I kept murmuring the name of Jesus over and over. The elder said to me, rather abruptly, 'Forget about Jesus!' The pastor said to me, 'Do you remember how, after the resurrection, Jesus appeared to his disciples and "breathed upon them, and said unto them, receive ye the Holy Ghost . . ."? On the Day of Pentecost, what do you suppose the disciples did?' I knew the answer and said, 'I suppose they breathed in!' 'That's right! Now you start breathing in the Spirit.' I started to take deep breaths and immediately something began to happen to me. I had the growing sensation of 'pins and needles' all over my body, a strange numbness or tingling. I became locked in one position and could not move. My head was tilted backwards, my hands rested upon my knees and my mouth was locked into an O shape. I believed that the Holy Spirit had come upon me. I didn't speak in tongues at that time, but a few days later found that I could babble a few meaningless sounds; this I took to be tongues. My wife was very offended. Because she had not gone forward with me, people would not talk to her. Once I found that I could speak in tongues I used the gift in private prayer. Some people claim that it is an overwhelming gift or that it fills them with ecstasy, but I never found it so. However, I could easily speak in tongues for great lengths of time. I did not find my spiritual life improved to any great extent, but the experience did create in me a feeling of superiority over those who had not received the gift.

As I gained more experience of charismatic meetings I began to prophesy. Usually this consisted of saying encouraging things to the meeting, prefaced with 'Thus saith the Lord'.

I have always had a vivid imagination and tend to think in pictures. I was encouraged by others to believe that these mental pictures were visions from God. I launched out and started to share these visions in meetings. For example, a stream flowing through a meadow. The stream is sluggish and filled with twigs and rubbish, which hinder the flow of the water. A hand came down and scooped out the dirt and twigs and the water flowed clear and bright again. The interpretation of the vision was that if we would allow him to, God would cleanse our lives and our Christian lives would be stronger as the Holy Spirit was allowed to use us.

By the late 1960s a small group had been built up in the part of the City of London where I worked. In this group I had some influence. I organized various meetings and became something of a minister; people expected me to pray, prophesy or to say something edifying. I was reading the Bible regularly and praying for hours each day, sometimes up to four hours. What I read in Scripture was passed on as 'revelation' from the Lord.

In the late 1960s I began to be influenced by Pentecostal/ holiness teaching. The euphoria of the 'baptism in the Holy Spirit' had faded over the years and I needed a new experience. The teaching by which I was influenced told me that I could come into a position of perfection (that is, I could choose not to sin). I was taught that the doctrine of the new birth as taught by most Christian groups was very inadequate (a view probably held by most evangelical believers, though for rather different reasons). Having been exposed to this teaching, I gradually came to the conclusion that, because my spiritual life was so inadequate (in spite of my 'Spirit-baptism'), I had never really been born again. This troubled me greatly and I sought the Lord in prayer. In November 1969 I seemed to grasp hold of Jesus in a new

way; I started to date my new birth from this time. I did
find for a time that my spiritual life improved and I believed
that I had victory over sin — or was I fooling myself? However, it did not last.

In the early 1970s I came into contact with a man who
claimed that he had a remarkable prayer life and that the Lord
used him in the healing of many people. This man taught
that for the Christian to know blessing he should stop using
his mind, the mind being totally evil and unregenerate. My
wife and I and another man, who was a close friend, developed
a close friendship with this man and we were convinced he
was a man of God. He told us how much he had been used
by God in the healing ministry (on one occasion raising a
little girl from the dead), but we never saw any proof of
this ministry. A number of things he said and did caused
us to begin to question whether he was all he seemed to be.
In the space of two years we had come to the sad conclusion
that he was a charlatan. He is still (as far as we know)
'ministering' all over the world and no doubt bringing other
gullible souls into bondage.

Over the next few years, partly because I was not a member
of a church or group, I gradually became more and more disillusioned with what I knew of the charismatic movement.
The way that charismatic people lived didn't seem to match
with the scriptural idea of what a Christian was and how he
should behave. Charismatics seemed to 'act a part'. There
was the charismatic voice, the dramatic posture, the
impression of super-spirituality. All these things seemed to
point to the fact that some people's experience of the Lord
was not all it should have been.

The way some people behaved was extremely odd. One
couple I got in touch with invited my wife and me to tea.
I explained that my wife was likely to be upset by any heavy-
handed approach to her and had extracted a promise that
their behaviour would be very gentle. Almost as soon as we
arrived at the house I was taken into the garden where the
husband, myself and assorted children played a game of

cricket. Joan was led upstairs to see the 'sanctuary' (a room set aside for prayer) and as soon as she was inside, she was pushed into a chair and held there while the woman of the house proceeded to 'cast out demons'. Needless to say, we left rather more rapidly than we came. This couple have since gained some influence among charismatics in the Medway Towns.

The man spoken of earlier (the man with the healing and prayer ministry) had been to see Kathryn Kuhlmann in the U.S.A. and had noted how some people had been 'slain by the Spirit' under her ministry (a number of people who had been ministered to by her, and had hands laid on them, fell to the ground. This is referred to in charismatic circles as 'being slain in or by the Spirit'). Our friend had been very impressed by this and endeavoured to bring it into his own ministry. But the only way he could emulate it was by physically pushing people over. I know, for he tried to do it to me.

Another thing which drew me away from the movement (should I say, drove me away?) were the noisy meetings, where everyone present spoke, sang or shouted in tongues or just prayed out loud. In a meeting where a hundred or more people are gathered this can become very noisy indeed.

By the mid 1970s my disillusionment had increased to such an extent that I had resigned from all my previously held positions of responsibility. I was not attending any church and only going to occasional meetings in my lunch hour. I had even stopped reading the Scriptures and only prayed in fits and starts.

Due to a personal crisis in my life, I began to see that my spiritual life was a mess and I came under considerable conviction of sin. This prompted me to start praying again in earnest, though I found it extremely difficult. I also took up my Bible reading again and renewed my pattern of daily reading.

My dabblings with error were not over yet, however. Such was my weak condition that I was infected with the Oxford Group movement's 'wait and see' teaching (see Appendix).

I would get up early each morning and wait with notebook and pencil to receive a 'message'. This I would write down and regard as my 'orders for the day', so to speak. Usually what came was not very specific on doing things; it was very much like most prophecy in the charismatic movement. This error lasted until I discovered that non-Christians and occultists used the same technique.

In 1979 while I was travelling with a friend, he mentioned the subject of 'Calvinism'. I asked him to explain and he took me quickly through the acrostic 'TULIP'.[11] As he explained each point, I had to admit that this was an adequate summary of what I had come to believe. It was a curious experience. Not so many years before I had preached against Calvinism (and every other -ism) and yet here I was confronted with the fact that unwittingly, in a sense against my will, I had come to believe Calvinist doctrine. During the next few weeks I followed this up with some specific reading on Calvinism. I came to see that if all are called to be saved, then God has failed; but if God has called only a specific number, the elect, then he has gloriously triumphed, for these will be called and they will respond to that call.

I saw clearly that if God had left the choice of whether I would follow Jesus or not entirely to me, then I would never have become a Christian. But because in his plan my salvation was essential, then God made sure that I responded to his call. I came to appreciate why Paul had called himself a prisoner of the Lord (Ephesians 3:1): not simply because he was in a Roman prison, but because the Lord had captured him and would never release him. For the Christian has received a life sentence, from which he can never be released, for which we continually give thanks.

At this time I also saw how deeply into error I had fallen and I found myself mourning over this. I reread Walter Chantry's *Signs of the Apostles* at this time and was especially convicted as I read James Davenport's confession: 'I confess I have been much led astray by following impulses and impressions as a rule of conduct, whether they came with or without a text of Scripture; I am persuaded this was a great means of corrupting my experiences and carrying me off from the Word of God, and a great handle, which the false spirit has made use of with respect to a number, and me especially.' I remember vividly blushing to the roots of my hair when I read this, for it summed up my own feelings so well. I had led others into the same error I had been in; I had encouraged people to use charismatic gifts.

Over the next few months I endeavoured to speak to a number of those whom I had influenced or had fellowship with in the past. Only one brother has taken any notice of my testimony, most considering that I had now fallen into error. One friend who had been a great encouragement and help to me over a number of years has gone so far as to tell me that he does not consider that I am born again.

Nevertheless I realize as never before how good the Lord has been to me, in calling me out of the charismatic movement. No doubt I will make many more mistakes before I finally see him face to face, but 'I am convinced that he is able to guard what I have entrusted to him for that day'.

To the name of the Lord Jesus Christ be all the glory!

18.
Conclusion

What then, is the Christian to make of this group of people, who claim special miracles and revelations from God, who claim a special relationship with him because of this second experience of the 'baptism in the Spirit', who claim that God is moving today in an end-time revival of the New Testament gifts?

There are many sincere, born-again believers in the ranks of the charismatic movement. But what do we make of a group whose claims of miracles are exaggerated, many of whose healings are at best psychological, whose tongues are gibberish and not languages, and whose behaviour is often eccentric and extreme?

It is my contention that part of the blame for the upsurge of this movement is the failure of modern evangelicalism. We have a low view of God and a low view of his Word, the Bible. As A. W. Tozer has said, 'The Church has surrendered her once lofty concept of God and has substituted for it one so low, so ignoble, as to be utterly unworthy of thinking, worshipping men.'[1] In the same book he continues, 'A right conception of God is basic, not only to systematic theology but to practical Christian living as well. It is to worship what the foundation is to the temple; where it is inadequate or out of plumb the whole structure must sooner or later collapse. I believe there is scarcely an error in doctrine or a failure in applying Christian ethics that cannot be traced finally to imperfect or ignoble thoughts about God.

'It is my opinion that the Christian conception of God

current in these middle years of the twentieth century is so decadent as to be utterly beneath the dignity of the Most High God and actually to constitute for professed believers something amounting to a moral calamity.'[2]

Evangelicalism has been much affected by Arminianism and decisionism. The concept of the ABC way to Christ (*A*sk Jesus into your heart; *B*elieve that he has come in; *C*onfess with your lips your new faith), has become so widely accepted as to be almost universal. How many people do we see, in this day and age, who show real concern over their spiritual condition, who will not be satisfied or fobbed off with easy answers to their questions, until they *know* that God in Christ has found them?

The evangelical view of sanctification was, in the last century, very much influenced by the so-called 'higher life movement'. This opened up the way for Pentecostalism and the charismatic movement by insisting that there were two classes of Christians — the carnal and the spiritual. There was a second experience for the Christian which shifted him onto a higher plane and made him into a spiritual man. This teaching inevitably led on to the search for experience. Whilst we recognize that the Christian must experience the Lord and his grace, this is not to say that experiences are the be-all and end-all of the spiritual life.

Another major influence has been dispensationalism, which sliced up the Scriptures, making large parts inapplicable to the church and also encouraged people to look for the 'signs of the times'.

These strands, together with much else, have been woven into the modern charismatic movement.

Christianity must return to the Scriptures, to 'teaching, rebuking, correcting and training in righteousness, so that the man of God may be thoroughly equipped' for service (2 Timothy 3:16, 17).

We must return to the preaching of the whole will of God — especially, in view of their recent neglect, to those doctrines known as the 'doctrines of grace'. We must insist that sanctification is an essential part of the Christian life, not an optional extra for those who feel the desire for it.

At the same time let us take a firm stand against the charismatic movement. This movement is here to stay and we will not make it go away by pretending it isn't there. We will also have no effect on it if we take the line, as some evangelicals have, that 'It's all right for those who feel the need for it'. The movement is either right or wrong. If it is right, then *all* of us should be seeking after gifts and ministering them in the church. If it is wrong, then *all* of us should make some kind of stand against it.

Let us pray for revival (we certainly need it in this last quarter of the twentieth century), a true outpouring of the Spirit of God, that we ourselves may be enlightened and enriched and that many who now claim to be 'filled with the Spirit' may also have their eyes and their hearts opened to the greatness of our God.

Appendix

Appendix

Quoted below are sample entries from my notebook, compared with the daily guidance received from Mrs Eileen Caddy. These extracts are taken from Mrs Caddy's book *God Spoke To Me*, published by the Findhorn Foundation in 1971. Accompanying these extracts are entries from *God Calling (A Devotional Diary)* by two listeners.[1]

The Findhorn community was founded by Mrs Caddy and her husband Peter (a former hotel manager), in Moray, Scotland. On a piece of semi-derelict land they have built a community around the guidance of Mrs Caddy. She spends long hours sitting with a notebook waiting for guidance, which she writes down. The community grows vegetables and has become well known for the size and quality of these. The community believes that the reason for their success is that they co-operate with the devas (i.e. spirits which help plants to grow; they claim that some of their number can communicate with these devas and with elves). The community is clearly based on contact with supernatural and occult powers. Its gospel, which is 'another gospel', is universalist and may be summed up in this extract: 'Stop and look at those around you and let your heart be filled with gratitude. When all are united in their highest beliefs (no matter what their beliefs, creed, sect or colour), you see the true brotherhood of man because you know that I AM the true Fatherhood of Man — all are one in Me and there is no separation.'[2]

The book *God Calling, by two listeners* is the product

of two anonymous ladies who tried to find guidance from
God in this same way – sitting with notebook and pencil,
waiting for 'the voice of God'. This book was first published
in 1935 and world sales are reputed to be 750,000. This
book is used for daily reading by a good number of people.

One of the women wrote a chapter on how they received
their guidance. She remarks how unworthy they felt at
receiving guidance in this way '. . . when millions of souls
had to be content with guidance from the Bible, sermons,
their Churches, books and other sources'.[3] And she goes
on to say that 'To use this book, which we believe has been
guided by our Lord Himself, is no ordinary book.'[4] 'It is
published, after much prayer, to prove that a living Christ
speaks today . . .'[5]. So we can see the implication that this
form of guidance is *superior* to guidance from Scripture.

Sample extracts

God Spoke to Me: 'Your close relationship with Me is more
important than anything else, for all stems from that relationship. The more time you spend with Me, the smoother will
be the running of your everyday living. From that centre,
where you will always find Me when you seek, the ripples
go out in ever increasing power. I AM your guide. I AM
your God' (p. 19).

God Calling: 'Walk with Me, I will teach you. Listen to Me
and I will speak. Continue to meet Me, in spite of all
opposition and every obstacle, in spite of days when you
may hear no voice, and there may come no intimate heart-
to-heart talking' (p. 45).

Author's Notebook: 'I will walk with you. Where you go
I am there too, for I am within you. I fill your heart with My
invisible light. I walk in you. Walk in Me. Fear Me and obey
Me as you should. Do My will always.'

God Spoke to Me: 'My Word is the Bread of Life. Therefore, whenever you are hungry, be still and receive the Bread of Life which gives life eternal.

'Many wonders will be seen with the physical eye, but even greater wonders by the eye of the Spirit. This is barred from none, but the desire must be great' (p. 24).

God Calling: 'I am with you. My presence is a sign of My forgiveness. I uphold you.

'You will conquer. Do not fear changes. You can never fear change when I, your Lord, change not. Jesus Christ, the same yesterday, today and forever. I am beside you. Steadfastness, unchangingness, come to you, too, as you dwell in Me. Rest in Me' (p. 99).

Author's Notebook: 'I am with you to guide you and I will sustain you day by day. I will give you your daily bread, and feed you. Do not be anxious. Walk in my Spirit now, walk with Me.'

God Spoke to Me: 'Always remember that I AM the Vine and you are the branches. I AM the source of All. You can do all things through Me but without Me you are nothing. With Me you are all things and can do all things. Never separate yourselves from Me in thought, word or deed. Seek that complete Oneness with Me and abide in it for ever and ever.

'Abide in Me and I in you and know that great shall be the works that you shall do in My Name. Miracle upon miracle shall come about. The light shall shine forth for all to see and they shall be drawn to the light and shall abide in the light and there shall be no darkness' (p. 95).

God Calling: 'I lead you. The way is clear. Go forward unafraid. I am beside you. Listen, listen, listen to My Voice. My hand is controlling all.

'Remember that I can work through you better when you are at rest. Go very slowly, very quietly from one duty to the next — taking time to rest and pray in between.

'Know that you can do all things through Christ who strengthens you. Nay, more, know that you can do all things through Christ who rests you' (p. 115).

Author's Notebook: 'Don't be anxious about tomorrow. I will take care of you. You are my children and a father always takes care of his children, doesn't he? I won't let you down. You will follow Me and My love will protect you. My spirit will go with you and guide you. Don't be anxious, don't keep looking ahead. Just live today and let Me take care of tomorrow.'

These extracts should be sufficient to show the uncomfortable similarity between occult guidance and guidance received in a charismatic way. These extracts are very similar to prophecies uttered in charismatic meetings. They should act as a warning to any who have fallen into this form of receiving guidance and also to any who read *God Calling* as if it was the Word of God.

Notes

Notes

Chapter 2

1. See Robert Gromacki, *The Modern Tongues Movement,* Presbyterian and Reformed Publishing Co., 1967, revised 1972, p. 6.
2. An oracle was a shrine at which enquiries would be made of the god or hero to whom the shrine was dedicated. Each oracle had its priests, priestesses and helpers. The commonest methods of obtaining answers were
   a. *Incubation,* when the enquirer slept in the shrine and received the answer in a dream;
   b. *Divination,* by lot. This took place with slivers of wood inscribed with antique letters. The slivers were stirred and one was pulled out by a boy employed by the oracle;
   c. *Direct enquiry* of an inspired person who answered orally.
3. John P. Kildahl, *The Psychology of Speaking in Tongues,* Hodder and Stoughton, 1972, p. 11.
4. 'Python was originally the name of the great soothsaying serpent of Delphi, which was killed by Apollo. Hence the god took his title of Pythius, and became the inspirer of oracles and soothsayers. His priestess at Delphi was called Pythia or Pythonissa; latterly the term Python was transferred to any soothsaying demon which gave responses in the name of Apollo' (G. H. Pember, M.A., *Earth's Earliest Ages,* Pickering and Inglis, p. 278).
   The slave girl referred to in Acts 16:16 had a spirit of Python (cf. Greek New Testament). The girl, no doubt a devotee of Apollo, was possessed by a Pythonic spirit and her owners probably made their money through divination and fortune-telling. The Pythonic spirit would often put the medium into a trance.
5. *Encyclopaedia Britannica,* 1966 ed., vol. 16.
6. *Modern Tongues Movement,* pp. 7–8.
7. As above.
8. *Earth's Earliest Ages,* pp. 285–288.
9. *Modern Tongues Movement,* pp. 6–7.
10. *Psychology of Speaking in Tongues,* p. 11.

11. Professor S. Angus, *The Mystery Religions,* Dover Publications (New York), 1975, pp. 100–101, quoted in John F. MacArthur, *The Charismatics – a doctrinal perspective,* Lamp Press, 1979, p. 111.
12. J. N. Darby, *The Holy Bible – A New Translation,* Stow Hill Bible and Tract Depot, 1871.

Chapter 4

1. *Modern Tongues Movement,* p. 12.
2. B. B. Warfield, *Counterfeit Miracles,* Banner of Truth Trust, pp. 299–300.
3. *Encyclopaedia Britannica,* vol. 22.
4. Eusebius, quoted in *Modern Tongues Movement,* p. 13.
5. *Psychology of Speaking in Tongues,* p. 15.
6. David Christie-Murray, *Voices From the Gods – Speaking in Tongues,* Routledge & Keegan Paul, 1978, p. 37.
7. *Modern Tongues Movement,* p. 16.
8. As above, p. 17.
9. *Counterfeit Miracles,* p. 41.
10. *Psychology of Speaking in Tongues,* p. 15.
11. Augustine, *The City of God,* Penguin, pp. 1033–1049.
12. *Voices From the Gods,* p. 38 and *Modern Tongues Movement,* p. 18.
13. *Encyclopaedia Britannica,* vol. 13, p. 2; John Henry Blunt (ed.), *Dictionary of Sects, Heresies and Ecclesiastical Parties and Schools of Religious Thought,* Longmans, Green & Co., 1903, p. 241.
14. *Counterfeit Miracles,* p. 89.
15. *Voices From the Gods,* p. 38.
16. As above.
17. Ullman, *The Reformers Before the Reformation,* quoted in *Dictionary of Sects,* p. 69.
18. *Dictionary of Sects,* p. 621.
19. *Modern Tongues Movement,* p. 18.
20. As above, p. 19.
21. Michael Harper, *As at the Beginning,* Hodder & Stoughton, 7th impression, 1975, p. 20.
22. *Voices From the Gods,* p. 40.
23. *Dictionary of Sects,* p. 1.
24. As above, p. 158.
25. *Modern Tongues Movement,* p. 21, and William C. Braithwaite, *The Beginnings of Quakerism,* MacMillan & Co. Ltd, 1972, pp. 289–293.
26. *Modern Tongues Movement,* p. 21.
27. *Voices From the Gods,* p. 44.
28. *Dictionary of Sects,* p. 112.

29. As above, p. 100.
30. As above; *Modern Tongues Movement*, pp. 20–21; *Voices From the Gods*, pp. 46–50.
31. *As at the Beginning*, pp. 19–20.
32. John Wesley, *A Plain Account of Christian Perfection*, Epworth Press, p. 59.
33. Cecil Roth and Geoffrey Wigoder (eds.), *New Standard Jewish Encyclopaedia*, W. H. Allen, 1975, pp. 209–212.
34. Walter Chantry, *Signs of the Apostles*, Banner of Truth Trust, 2nd ed., 1976, pp. 134–136.
35. *The Narrative of Jonathan Edwards* (abridged edition), Revival Literature, p. 34.
36. Joseph Tracey, *The Great Awakening*, Banner of Truth Trust, p. 250, quoted in *Signs of the Apostles*, p. 132.
37. *Dwight's Travels*, quoted in *Dictionary of Sects*, p. 558.
38. *Dictionary of Sects*, p. 558.
39. *Voices From the Gods*, p. 53.
40. *Story's Life of Story*, p. 205, quoted in *Dictionary of Sects*, p. 227.
41. *Dictionary of Sects*, p. 227.
42. *Voices From the Gods*, p. 58.
43. J. Barton Payne, *The Imminent Appearing of Christ*, Wm. B. Edmons Publications Co., 1962, p. 32.
44. Oliphant's *Life of Irving*, vol. ii, pp. 223–225, quoted in *Dictionary of Sects*, p. 227.
45. Quoted in *Voices From the Gods*, p. 59.
46. *Voices From the Gods*, p. 60.
47. As above, p. 64.
48. Quoted in *The Best of Andrew Murray*, Baker Book House, p. 86.
49. *The Best of Andrew Murray*, pp. 126–127.
50. *Metropolitan Tabernacle Pulpit*, vol. 23, p. 471, quoted in *Signs of the Apostles*, p. 91.
51. Demos Shakarian, *The Happiest People on Earth*, Hodder & Stoughton, 1975, p. 20.
52. As above, p. 36.
53. As above, p. 20.
54. *As at the Beginning*, p. 72.
55. *Modern Tongues Movement*, pp. 25–26.

Chapter 5

1. It is reported that the Eskimos of Greenland have religious meetings which are 'characterized by drum-beating, singing, dancing, and nudity of both men and women. During these meetings speaking in tongues also occurs' (*Modern Tongues Movement*, p. 9).

2. *Voices From the Gods,* pp. 5, 6, 7, 10.
3. V. R. Edman, quoted in *Modern Tongues Movement,* p. 9.
4. *Earth's Earliest Ages,* pp. 316–318.
5. *Voices From the Gods,* p. 70.

Chapter 6

1. *Modern Tongues Movement,* p. 26, and *As at the Beginning,* pp. 26–27.
2. Arno Gaebelain, quoted in *Modern Tongues Movement,* p. 26.
3. *As at the Beginning,* pp. 31–32.
4. *Voices From the Gods,* pp. 101–102.
5. *As at the Beginning,* pp. 36–41.
6. As above, pp. 42–44.
7. As above, pp. 43–46.
8. *Voices From the Gods,* p. 104.
9. As above, p. 104.
10. As above.
11. As above, p. 105.
12. As above.
13. As above, p. 107.
14. See cover, Dr Paul Yonggi Cho, *The Fourth Dimension,* Logos International, 1979.

Chapter 7

1. Harold Bredesen, quoted in *Modern Tongues Movement,* p. 45.
2. *Happiest People on Earth,* p. 127.
3. As above, p. 128.
4. *As at the Beginning,* pp. 80–81.
5. As above, pp. 60–70.
6. As above, p. 76.
7. *Modern Tongues Movement,* p. 163.
8. *As at the Beginning,* pp. 80–84.
9. As above, p. 81.
10. David du Plessis is a South African, former Assemblies of God minister, now speaking widely among charismatic groups all over the world. He has been to the World Council of Churches with the charismatic message. These men were impressed with him because he refused to talk about doctrine, which he knew would divide them, but spoke of experience. See his book *The Spirit Bade Me Go,* Logos International.

11. Larry Christensen is a Lutheran pastor from the U.S.A. who has ministered widely to charismatic groups in the U.S.A. and United Kingdom. He has written a number of books on various aspects of the charismatic movement.
12. *As at the Beginning,* pp. 84–86.
13. *Crusade* is the official magazine of the Evangelical Alliance, now called *Today.*
14. *As at the Beginning,* p. 87.
15. Michael Harper, *This is the Day,* Hodder & Stoughton, 1979, p. 35.
16. As above, p. 51.
17. *Modern Tongues Movement,* p. 153.
18. *Happiest People on Earth,* p. 156.
19. As above.
20. *This is the Day,* p. 31.
21. As above, p. 33.
22. As above, p. 39.
23. Juan Carlos Ortiz, *Disciple,* p. 62.
24. Derek Prince, *Discipleship, Shepherding, Commitment,* Derek Prince Publications, 1976, p. 20.
25. The teaching over water baptism was that, even if the Christian had been baptized in the name of the Father, the Son and the Holy Ghost by total immersion, he must be re-baptized in the name of Jesus only. This led to a number of break-away groups, meeting under the name of 'Jesus only'.
26. Merlin Carrothers, *Prison to Praise, Power through Praise, Walking and Leaping.*

Chapter 8

1. *Christianity Today,* 21, no. 10 (18 February 1977), p. 18.
2. American slang term for prostitute.
3. *Restoration,* May/June 1981, p. 15.
4. J. I. Packer, *Keep in Step with the Spirit,* IVP.
5. *Evangelical Times,* January 1982.
6. *Time* magazine, 8 November 1982.
7. Martha Zimmerman, *Celebrate the Feasts of the Old Testament in your own Home or Church,* Bethany House Publishing, 1981.
8. See Gerald Coates, *What on Earth is this Kingdom?* Kingsway Publications.
9. Steve Lightle, *Exodus II,* p. 184.

Chapter 9

1. *Journal of George Fox,* revised John L. Nickalls, Religious Society of Friends, 1975, p. 688.

Chapter 10

1. James Naylor was an early Quaker who was persuaded (partly by female followers, partly by his own poor mental and spiritual condition) that he was Christ. He rode into Bristol on a horse, his followers throwing their clothes in his pathway in a re-enactment of Jesus' entry into Jerusalem. The vast majority of the early Quakers, including George Fox, condemned him. He was later charged with blasphemy by the authorities and, when found guilty, had his tongue bored through with a hot iron. He repented of his folly and was reconciled to Fox before he died, about three years later.
2. *The Beginnings of Quakerism,* p. 243.
3. As above, p. 290.
4. G. W. North, *Spiritual Life and Spiritual Gifts,* Part II, 'The Spirituals', p. 20. G. W. North is an independent Bible teacher who ministers among a number of fellowships up and down the United Kingdom. His teachings differ from the main-line charismatics, inasmuch as he states that new birth and baptism of the Holy Spirit are the same experience. He teaches Christian perfection. He is not widely accepted in charismatic circles (so is not representative of the movement generally) and he has a poor view of the charismatic movement.
5. *The Eden Bible.*
6. Catherine Marshall, *Something More,* p. 281.
7. *Peace and Truth,* 1978, no. 4, an article entitled 'Prisoner of the Book' by Michael Buss, p. 10.
8. *The Charismatics,* p. 10.
9. As above, p. 20.
10. *The Spirit Bade Me Go,* p. 9.
11. For a fuller and better treatment of this theme see *Signs of the Apostles* and *The Charismatics.*
12. *Banner of Truth,* March 1979, pp. 24–25.
13. Andrew Woolsey, *Duncan Campbell – A Biography,* Hodder & Stoughton, p. 118.

Chapter 11

1. *The Charismatics,* p. 11.
2. As above, p. 137.
3. As above, p. 140.
4. As above, p. 136.
5. As above, p. 138.
6. St Marks, Gillingham, Kent is an Anglican church which was influenced during the early 1960s. Rev. John Collins was the vicar during the church's most fruitful period.
7. From *Revival,* April 1973, quoted in *Peace and Truth,* 1979, no. 2, p. 13.
8. Quoted in *Modern Tongues Movement,* p. 112.
9. Stanley H. Frodsham, *With Signs Following,* 1926, pp. 242–243.
10. *Psychology of Speaking in Tongues,* p. 24.
11. George E. Gardiner, *The Corinthian Catastrophe,* Kregel Publications, 5th printing, 1977.
12. Quoted in *Modern Tongues Movement,* p. 66.
13. *Voices From the Gods,* p. 171.
14. Glossolalia, derived from the Greek words *'glossa'* (the tongue) and *'lalien'* (to talk), literally, 'to speak with the tongue'. In the New Testament it denotes a language spoken by someone with no previous knowledge of that language. Here, of course, it refers to the modern phenomenon.
15. Quoted in *The Charismatics,* p. 162.
16. *The Psychology of Speaking in Tongues,* p. 27.
17. Donald Gee, *Concerning Spiritual Gifts,* The Gospel Publishing House, p. 96.
18. *Psychology of Speaking in Tongues,* pp. 2, 3.
19. As above, pp. 72–73.
20. Quoted in *Modern Tongues Movement,* p. 41.
21. As above, p. 42.
22. *Psychology of Speaking in Tongues,* p. 63.
23. Quoted in *Modern Tongues Movement,* p. 114.

Chapter 12

1. *Modern Tongues Movement,* p. 16. Also, Donald W. Burdick, *Tongues, to Speak or Not to Speak,* Moody Press, 1969, p. 33.
2. *The Charismatics,* p. 166.
3. *As at the Beginning,* p. 19.

Chapter 13

1. For the full account of this remarkable incident see *The Happiest People on Earth*, pp. 20, 36.
2. 'When you come together . . . If anyone speaks in a tongue, two — or at the most three — should speak, one at a time, and someone must interpret. If there is no interpreter, the speaker should keep quiet in the church and speak to himself and God' (1 Corinthians 14:26–28).
3. *The Happiest People on Earth*, p. 25.
4. *Psychology of Speaking in Tongues*, p. 61.
5. The Oxford Group movement was started by Lutheran Frank Buchman in the early half of the century. He emphasized the four absolutes — absolute honesty, absolute purity, absolute unselfishness and absolute love. Because of this emphasis he tended to minimize the atonement and the central place of the Saviour, the Lord Jesus Christ. As time went on, the gap between orthodox Christianity and the Oxford Group became more and more pronounced. By the time it changed its name to Moral Re-armament (M.R.A.) it had dropped any pretence of being a Christian movement. It is not to be confused with the Oxford Movement.
6. Dr Kenneth McCall to the Lloyds Christian Union (taped).
7. Kenneth E. Hagin, *I Believe in Visions*, Fleming H. Revell, 1972.

Chapter 14

1. For a fuller treatment of this theme see *Reformation Today*, no. 83 (January/March 1985), 'Studies in Biblical Theology — The progress of Revelation in the New Testament, Part III'.
2. *Psychology of Speaking in Tongues*, p. 2.
3. As above, p. 5.
4. As above, p. 6.
5. *Modern Tongues Movement*, p. 151.
6. *Happiest People on Earth*, p. 38.
7. *Peace and Truth*, 1978, no. 4, p. 5.

Chapter 15

1. *This is the Day*, p. 43.
2. As above.
3. As above, p. 112.

4. *Peace and Truth,* 1979, no. 1, p. 9, quoting the *Bible League Quarterly,* p. 185.
5. M. Malinski, trans. P. S. Falla, *Pope John Paul II – The Life of my Friend Karol Wojtyla,* Burns & Oates, 1979, p. 5.
6. *This is the Day,* p. 31.
7. As above, p. 30.
8. *Modern Tongues Movement,* p. 156.
9. As above.
10. As above.
11. As above.

Chapter 16

1. *Duncan Campbell,* p. 121.
2. Emyr Roberts and R. Geraint Gruffydd, *Revival and Its Fruit,* Evangelical Press of Wales, 1981, p. 4.
3. *Peace and Truth,* 1981, no. 1, p. 8.
4. As above.
5. *Duncan Campbell,* p. 121.
6. As above, pp. 121–122.
7. *The Narrative;* p. 25.
8. As above, p. 37.
9. *Duncan Campbell,* p. 128.
10. William Blair and Bruce Hunt, *The Korean Pentecost and the Sufferings which Followed,* Banner of Truth Trust, 1977, pp. 76–77.
11. As above.
12. As above, p. 8.
13. There are some ways in which the Welsh Revival of 1904 was different from other revivals. The over-emphasis on singing and the consequently lower place given to preaching was one area. Evan Roberts also had strange ideas regarding the coming of the Holy Spirit. He used to ask the congregation to repeat a prayer, requesting the descent of the Spirit, over and over again. He was also in correspondence with men of a Pentecostal outlook and seems to have had a great deal of sympathy with them.
14. *Revival and its Fruit,* p. 9.
15. *The Narrative,* p. 27.
16. As above, pp. 65–66.
17. David Pawson tape.
18. *Revival and its Fruit,* p. 20, etc.
19. *The Fourth Dimension,* pp. 18–21.

Chapter 17

1. The facts for this section have been gleaned from J. F. Thornbury, *God Sent Revival – The Story of Asahel Nettleton and the Second Great Awakening,* Evangelical Press, 1977, pp. 48–51, and *The Great Awakening,* pp. 230–255.
2. Facts have been gleaned from H. A. Ironside, Litt. D., *Holiness – The False and the True,* Liozeaux Bros. Inc., 1912, 23rd imp. 1980.
3. Wong Ming-Dao, *A Stone Made Smooth,* Mayflower Christian Books, 1981, pp. 2–3.
4. As above, p. 65.
5. As above.
6. As above, pp. 69–74.
7. As above, p. 83.
8. As above, pp. 82–83.
9. Facts gleaned from the introduction to *The Corinthian Catastrophe,* pp. 7–10.
10. Gleaned from an article in *Peace and Truth,* 1978, no. 4, pp. 5–7.
11. Total depravity
    Unconditional election
    Limited atonement
    Irresistible grace
    Perseverance of the saints.

Chapter 18

1. A. W. Tozer, *The Knowledge of the Holy,* STL Productions, 1977, p. 6.
2. As above, p. 10.

Appendix

1. A. J. Russell (ed.), *God Calling (A Devotional Diary) – by Two Listeners,* Arthur James Ltd.
2. *God Spoke to Me,* p. 97.
3. *God Calling,* p. 14.
4. As above, p. 16.
5. As above.

Bibliography

Bibliography

It is hoped that those who have read this brief work will go on to examine the work of the Holy Spirit in more detail. Shown here are a number of books which would be very helpful.

James Buchanan, *The Office and Work of the Holy Spirit*, Banner of Truth Trust (reprinted 1984).
Arthur W. Pink, *The Holy Spirit*, Baker Book House.

These two books are general works on the work of the Holy Spirit and are most helpful from the doctrinal point of view.

Walter Chantry, *Signs of the Apostles*, Banner of Truth Trust.
Robert Gromacki, *The Modern Tongues Movement*, Presbyterian & Reformed Publishing Co.
John F. MacArthur, *The Charismatics*, Zondervan Books.

These three books examine the charismatic movement and its teachings from a biblical perspective.

Erroll Hulse, *The Believer's Experience*, Carey Publications.

An examination of 'experience' and 'truth'.

George E. Gardiner, *The Corinthian Catastrophe,* Kregel Publications.

A brief look at the charismatic movement compared to the church at Corinth.

Arnold Dallimore, *The Life of Edward Irving,* Banner of Truth Trust.

This is an important book. Irving is looked upon by many as the forerunner of the charismatic movement.

Deborah Davis, *The Children of God,* Zondervan Books.

This book is included as it clearly illustrates the generation of a so-called spiritual movement. But be warned — don't read it unless you are prepared to be shocked!

Peter Masters, *Guidance,* Wakemans.

This work lays down clear teaching on an aspect of the Christian life which puzzles many 'young' Christians.

The Holy Spirit —
>   Proper Approach to Study   (TE–K–1)
>   Person, Necessity and Unity   (TE–K–2)
>   Glorification of Jesus Christ   (TE–K–3)
>   Relationship to the Scripture   (TE–K–4)

Four tapes from Al Martin on the work of the Holy Spirit. Available from: The Trinity Pulpit, Box 227, Essex Falls, New Jersey 07021.

These tapes would be very helpful for anyone seeking sound guidance regarding the person and work of the Holy Spirit.